Care Act 2014

CHAPTER 23

Explanatory Notes are available separately

GRAN*GIS* UK Publishing

Adapted and published by GRANGIS (Grand Register Library).
Online: www.grangis.com
E-mail: contact@grangis.com

In this version:
ISBN: 979-8-88559-008-2

Note: This is the original version (as it was originally enacted). Title, sub-title and the generated date is as marked on the pages.

Care Act 2014

CHAPTER 23

CARE ACT 2014

PART 1

CARE AND SUPPORT

General responsibilities of local authorities

Meeting needs for care etc.

Assessing needs

Charging and assessing financial resources

PART 2

CARE STANDARDS

Quality of services

Care Quality Commission

Increasing the independence of the Care Quality Commission

Performance ratings

False or misleading information

Regulated activities

PART 3

HEALTH

CHAPTER 1

HEALTH EDUCATION ENGLAND

Establishment

National functions

PART 4

HEALTH AND SOCIAL CARE

PART 5

GENERAL

6 Independent Health Care Regulations (Northern Ireland) 2005 (S.R. 2005/174)
7 Approval of Research on Organs No Longer Required for Procurator Fiscal Purposes (Specified Purposes) (Scotland) Order 2006 (S.S.I. 2006/310)
8 Human Tissue Act 2004 (Ethical Approval, Exceptions from Licensing and Supply of Information about Transplants) Regulations 2006 (S.I. 2006/1260)
9 Mental Capacity Act 2005 (Appropriate Body) (England) Regulations 2006 (S.I. 2006/2810)
10 Mental Capacity Act 2005 (Appropriate Body) (Wales) Regulations 2007 (S.I. 2007/833)
11 Human Fertilisation and Embryology (Disclosure of Information for Research Purposes) Regulations 2010 (S.I. 2010/995)
12 Independent Health Care (Wales) Regulations 2011 (S.I. 2011/734)

Care Act 2014

2014 CHAPTER 23

An Act to make provision to reform the law relating to care and support for adults and the law relating to support for carers; to make provision about safeguarding adults from abuse or neglect; to make provision about care standards; to establish and make provision about Health Education England; to establish and make provision about the Health Research Authority; to make provision about integrating care and support with health services; and for connected purposes. [14th May 2014]

BE IT ENACTED by the Queen's most Excellent Majesty, by and with the advice and consent of the Lords Spiritual and Temporal, and Commons, in this present Parliament assembled, and by the authority of the same, as follows:—

PART 1

CARE AND SUPPORT

General responsibilities of local authorities

1 Promoting individual well-being

(1) The general duty of a local authority, in exercising a function under this Part in the case of an individual, is to promote that individual's well-being.

(2) "Well-being", in relation to an individual, means that individual's well-being so far as relating to any of the following—

(a) personal dignity (including treatment of the individual with respect);

(b) physical and mental health and emotional well-being;

(c) protection from abuse and neglect;

(d) control by the individual over day-to-day life (including over care and support, or support, provided to the individual and the way in which it is provided);

(e) participation in work, education, training or recreation;

(f) social and economic well-being;
(g) domestic, family and personal relationships;
(h) suitability of living accommodation;
(i) the individual's contribution to society.

(3) In exercising a function under this Part in the case of an individual, a local authority must have regard to the following matters in particular—

(a) the importance of beginning with the assumption that the individual is best-placed to judge the individual's well-being;
(b) the individual's views, wishes, feelings and beliefs;
(c) the importance of preventing or delaying the development of needs for care and support or needs for support and the importance of reducing needs of either kind that already exist;
(d) the need to ensure that decisions about the individual are made having regard to all the individual's circumstances (and are not based only on the individual's age or appearance or any condition of the individual's or aspect of the individual's behaviour which might lead others to make unjustified assumptions about the individual's well-being);
(e) the importance of the individual participating as fully as possible in decisions relating to the exercise of the function concerned and being provided with the information and support necessary to enable the individual to participate;
(f) the importance of achieving a balance between the individual's well-being and that of any friends or relatives who are involved in caring for the individual;
(g) the need to protect people from abuse and neglect;
(h) the need to ensure that any restriction on the individual's rights or freedom of action that is involved in the exercise of the function is kept to the minimum necessary for achieving the purpose for which the function is being exercised.

(4) "Local authority" means—

(a) a county council in England,
(b) a district council for an area in England for which there is no county council,
(c) a London borough council, or
(d) the Common Council of the City of London.

2 Preventing needs for care and support

(1) A local authority must provide or arrange for the provision of services, facilities or resources, or take other steps, which it considers will—

(a) contribute towards preventing or delaying the development by adults in its area of needs for care and support;
(b) contribute towards preventing or delaying the development by carers in its area of needs for support;
(c) reduce the needs for care and support of adults in its area;
(d) reduce the needs for support of carers in its area.

(2) In performing that duty, a local authority must have regard to—

(a) the importance of identifying services, facilities and resources already available in the authority's area and the extent to which the authority could involve or make use of them in performing that duty;

(b) the importance of identifying adults in the authority's area with needs for care and support which are not being met (by the authority or otherwise);
(c) the importance of identifying carers in the authority's area with needs for support which are not being met (by the authority or otherwise).

(3) Regulations may—
(a) permit a local authority to make a charge for providing or arranging for the provision of services, facilities or resources, or for taking other steps, under this section;
(b) prohibit a local authority from making a charge it would otherwise be permitted to make by virtue of paragraph (a).

(4) The regulations may in particular (in reliance on section 125(7)) make provision by reference to services, facilities or resources which—
(a) are of a specified type;
(b) are provided in specified circumstances;
(c) are provided to an adult of a specified description;
(d) are provided for a specified period only.

(5) A charge under the regulations may cover only the cost that the local authority incurs in providing or arranging for the provision of the service, facility or resource or for taking the other step.

(6) In cases where a local authority performs the duty under subsection (1) jointly with one or more other local authorities in relation to the authorities' combined area—
(a) references in this section to a local authority are to be read as references to the authorities acting jointly, and
(b) references in this section to a local authority's area are to be read as references to the combined area.

(7) Sections 21 (exception for persons subject to immigration control), 22 (exception for provision of health services) and 23 (exception for provision of housing etc.) apply in relation to the duty under subsection (1), but with the modifications set out in those sections.

(8) "Adult" means a person aged 18 or over.

3 Promoting integration of care and support with health services etc.

(1) A local authority must exercise its functions under this Part with a view to ensuring the integration of care and support provision with health provision and health-related provision where it considers that this would—
(a) promote the well-being of adults in its area with needs for care and support and the well-being of carers in its area,
(b) contribute to the prevention or delay of the development by adults in its area of needs for care and support or the development by carers in its area of needs for support, or
(c) improve the quality of care and support for adults, and of support for carers, provided in its area (including the outcomes that are achieved from such provision).

(2) "Care and support provision" means—
(a) provision to meet adults' needs for care and support,

(b) provision to meet carers' needs for support, and

(c) provision of services, facilities or resources, or the taking of other steps, under section 2.

(3) "Health provision" means provision of health services as part of the health service.

(4) "Health-related provision" means provision of services which may have an effect on the health of individuals but which are not—

(a) health services provided as part of the health service, or

(b) services provided in the exercise of social services functions (as defined by section 1A of the Local Authority Social Services Act 1970).

(5) For the purposes of this section, the provision of housing is health-related provision.

(6) In section 13N of the National Health Service Act 2006 (duty of NHS Commissioning Board to promote integration), at the end insert—

"(5) For the purposes of this section, the provision of housing accommodation is a health-related service."

(7) In section 14Z1 of that Act (duty of clinical commissioning groups to promote integration), at the end insert—

"(4) For the purposes of this section, the provision of housing accommodation is a health-related service."

4 Providing information and advice

(1) A local authority must establish and maintain a service for providing people in its area with information and advice relating to care and support for adults and support for carers.

(2) The service must provide information and advice on the following matters in particular—

(a) the system provided for by this Part and how the system operates in the authority's area,

(b) the choice of types of care and support, and the choice of providers, available to those who are in the authority's area,

(c) how to access the care and support that is available,

(d) how to access independent financial advice on matters relevant to the meeting of needs for care and support, and

(e) how to raise concerns about the safety or well-being of an adult who has needs for care and support.

(3) In providing information and advice under this section, a local authority must in particular—

(a) have regard to the importance of identifying adults in the authority's area who would be likely to benefit from financial advice on matters relevant to the meeting of needs for care and support, and

(b) seek to ensure that what it provides is sufficient to enable adults—

(i) to identify matters that are or might be relevant to their personal financial position that could be affected by the system provided for by this Part,

(ii) to make plans for meeting needs for care and support that might arise, and

(iii) to understand the different ways in which they may access independent financial advice on matters relevant to the meeting of needs for care and support.

(4) Information and advice provided under this section must be accessible to, and proportionate to the needs of, those for whom it is being provided.

(5) "Independent financial advice" means financial advice provided by a person who is independent of the local authority in question.

(6) In cases where a local authority performs the duty under subsection (1) jointly with one or more other local authorities by establishing and maintaining a service for their combined area—

(a) references in this section to a local authority are to be read as references to the authorities acting jointly, and

(b) references in this section to a local authority's area are to be read as references to the combined area.

5 Promoting diversity and quality in provision of services

(1) A local authority must promote the efficient and effective operation of a market in services for meeting care and support needs with a view to ensuring that any person in its area wishing to access services in the market—

(a) has a variety of providers to choose from who (taken together) provide a variety of services;

(b) has a variety of high quality services to choose from;

(c) has sufficient information to make an informed decision about how to meet the needs in question.

(2) In performing that duty, a local authority must have regard to the following matters in particular—

(a) the need to ensure that the authority has, and makes available, information about the providers of services for meeting care and support needs and the types of services they provide;

(b) the need to ensure that it is aware of current and likely future demand for such services and to consider how providers might meet that demand;

(c) the importance of enabling adults with needs for care and support, and carers with needs for support, who wish to do so to participate in work, education or training;

(d) the importance of ensuring the sustainability of the market (in circumstances where it is operating effectively as well as in circumstances where it is not);

(e) the importance of fostering continuous improvement in the quality of such services and the efficiency and effectiveness with which such services are provided and of encouraging innovation in their provision;

(f) the importance of fostering a workforce whose members are able to ensure the delivery of high quality services (because, for example, they have relevant skills and appropriate working conditions).

(3) In having regard to the matters mentioned in subsection (2)(b), a local authority must also have regard to the need to ensure that sufficient services are available for meeting

the needs for care and support of adults in its area and the needs for support of carers in its area.

(4) In arranging for the provision by persons other than it of services for meeting care and support needs, a local authority must have regard to the importance of promoting the well-being of adults in its area with needs for care and support and the well-being of carers in its area.

(5) In meeting an adult's needs for care and support or a carer's needs for support, a local authority must have regard to its duty under subsection (1).

(6) In cases where a local authority performs the duty under subsection (1) jointly with one or more other local authorities in relation to persons who are in the authorities' combined area—

(a) references in this section to a local authority are to be read as references to the authorities acting jointly, and

(b) references in this section to a local authority's area are to be read as references to the combined area.

(7) "Services for meeting care and support needs" means—

(a) services for meeting adults' needs for care and support, and

(b) services for meeting carers' needs for support.

(8) The references in subsection (7) to services for meeting needs include a reference to services, facilities or resources the purpose of which is to contribute towards preventing or delaying the development of those needs.

6 Co-operating generally

(1) A local authority must co-operate with each of its relevant partners, and each relevant partner must co-operate with the authority, in the exercise of—

(a) their respective functions relating to adults with needs for care and support,

(b) their respective functions relating to carers, and

(c) functions of theirs the exercise of which is relevant to functions referred to in paragraph (a) or (b).

(2) A local authority must co-operate, in the exercise of its functions under this Part, with such other persons as it considers appropriate who exercise functions, or are engaged in activities, in the authority's area relating to adults with needs for care and support or relating to carers.

(3) The following are examples of persons with whom a local authority may consider it appropriate to co-operate for the purposes of subsection (2)—

(a) a person who provides services to meet adults' needs for care and support, services to meet carers' needs for support or services, facilities or resources of the kind referred to in section 2(1);

(b) a person who provides primary medical services, primary dental services, primary ophthalmic services, pharmaceutical services or local pharmaceutical services under the National Health Service Act 2006;

(c) a person in whom a hospital in England is vested which is not a health service hospital as defined by that Act;

(d) a private registered provider of social housing.

(4) A local authority must make arrangements for ensuring co-operation between—

(a) the officers of the authority who exercise the authority's functions relating to adults with needs for care and support or its functions relating to carers,

(b) the officers of the authority who exercise the authority's functions relating to housing (in so far as the exercise of those functions is relevant to functions referred to in paragraph (a)),

(c) the Director of Children's Services at the authority (in so far as the exercise of functions by that officer is relevant to the functions referred to in paragraph (a)), and

(d) the authority's director of public health (see section 73A of the National Health Service Act 2006).

(5) The references in subsections (1) and (4)(a) to a local authority's functions include a reference to the authority's functions under sections 58 to 65 (transition for children with needs etc.).

(6) The duties under subsections (1) to (4) are to be performed for the following purposes in particular—

(a) promoting the well-being of adults with needs for care and support and of carers in the authority's area,

(b) improving the quality of care and support for adults and support for carers provided in the authority's area (including the outcomes that are achieved from such provision),

(c) smoothing the transition to the system provided for by this Part for persons in relation to whom functions under sections 58 to 65 are exercisable,

(d) protecting adults with needs for care and support who are experiencing, or are at risk of, abuse or neglect, and

(e) identifying lessons to be learned from cases where adults with needs for care and support have experienced serious abuse or neglect and applying those lessons to future cases.

(7) Each of the following is a relevant partner of a local authority—

(a) where the authority is a county council for an area for which there are district councils, each district council;

(b) any local authority, or district council for an area in England for which there is a county council, with which the authority agrees it would be appropriate to co-operate under this section;

(c) each NHS body in the authority's area;

(d) the Minister of the Crown exercising functions in relation to social security, employment and training, so far as those functions are exercisable in relation to England;

(e) the chief officer of police for a police area the whole or part of which is in the authority's area;

(f) the Minister of the Crown exercising functions in relation to prisons, so far as those functions are exercisable in relation to England;

(g) a relevant provider of probation services in the authority's area;

(h) such person, or a person of such description, as regulations may specify.

(8) The reference to an NHS body in a local authority's area is a reference to—

(a) the National Health Service Commissioning Board, so far as its functions are exercisable in relation to the authority's area,

(b) a clinical commissioning group the whole or part of whose area is in the authority's arca, or

(c) an NHS trust or NHS foundation trust which provides services in the authority's area.

(9) "Prison" has the same meaning as in the Prison Act 1952 (see section 53(1) of that Act).

(10) "Relevant provider of probation services" has the meaning given by section 325 of the Criminal Justice Act 2003.

7 Co-operating in specific cases

(1) Where a local authority requests the co-operation of a relevant partner, or of a local authority which is not one of its relevant partners, in the exercise of a function under this Part in the case of an individual with needs for care and support or in the case of a carer, a carer of a child or a young carer, the partner or authority must comply with the request unless it considers that doing so—

(a) would be incompatible with its own duties, or

(b) would otherwise have an adverse effect on the exercise of its functions.

(2) Where a relevant partner of a local authority, or a local authority which is not one of its relevant partners, requests the co-operation of the local authority in its exercise of a function in the case of an individual with needs for care and support or in the case of a carer, a carer of a child or a young carer, the local authority must comply with the request unless it considers that doing so—

(a) would be incompatible with its own duties, or

(b) would otherwise have an adverse effect on the exercise of its functions.

(3) A person who decides not to comply with a request under subsection (1) or (2) must give the person who made the request written reasons for the decision.

(4) "Relevant partner", in relation to a local authority, has the same meaning as in section 6.

(5) "Carer of a child" means a person who is a carer for the purposes of section 60.

Meeting needs for care etc.

8 How to meet needs

(1) The following are examples of what may be provided to meet needs under sections 18 to 20—

(a) accommodation in a care home or in premises of some other type;

(b) care and support at home or in the community;

(c) counselling and other types of social work;

(d) goods and facilities;

(e) information, advice and advocacy.

(2) The following are examples of the ways in which a local authority may meet needs under sections 18 to 20—

(a) by arranging for a person other than it to provide a service;

(b) by itself providing a service;

(c) by making direct payments.

(3) "Care home" has the meaning given by section 3 of the Care Standards Act 2000.

Assessing needs

9 Assessment of an adult's needs for care and support

(1) Where it appears to a local authority that an adult may have needs for care and support, the authority must assess—

(a) whether the adult does have needs for care and support, and

(b) if the adult does, what those needs are.

(2) An assessment under subsection (1) is referred to in this Part as a "needs assessment".

(3) The duty to carry out a needs assessment applies regardless of the authority's view of—

(a) the level of the adult's needs for care and support, or

(b) the level of the adult's financial resources.

(4) A needs assessment must include an assessment of—

(a) the impact of the adult's needs for care and support on the matters specified in section 1(2),

(b) the outcomes that the adult wishes to achieve in day-to-day life, and

(c) whether, and if so to what extent, the provision of care and support could contribute to the achievement of those outcomes.

(5) A local authority, in carrying out a needs assessment, must involve—

(a) the adult,

(b) any carer that the adult has, and

(c) any person whom the adult asks the authority to involve or, where the adult lacks capacity to ask the authority to do that, any person who appears to the authority to be interested in the adult's welfare.

(6) When carrying out a needs assessment, a local authority must also consider—

(a) whether, and if so to what extent, matters other than the provision of care and support could contribute to the achievement of the outcomes that the adult wishes to achieve in day-to-day life, and

(b) whether the adult would benefit from the provision of anything under section 2 or 4 or of anything which might be available in the community.

(7) This section is subject to section 11(1) to (4) (refusal by adult of assessment).

10 Assessment of a carer's needs for support

(1) Where it appears to a local authority that a carer may have needs for support (whether currently or in the future), the authority must assess—

(a) whether the carer does have needs for support (or is likely to do so in the future), and

(b) if the carer does, what those needs are (or are likely to be in the future).

(2) An assessment under subsection (1) is referred to in this Part as a "carer's assessment".

(3) "Carer" means an adult who provides or intends to provide care for another adult (an "adult needing care"); but see subsections (9) and (10).

(4) The duty to carry out a carer's assessment applies regardless of the authority's view of—

(a) the level of the carer's needs for support, or

(b) the level of the carer's financial resources or of those of the adult needing care.

(5) A carer's assessment must include an assessment of—

(a) whether the carer is able, and is likely to continue to be able, to provide care for the adult needing care,

(b) whether the carer is willing, and is likely to continue to be willing, to do so,

(c) the impact of the carer's needs for support on the matters specified in section 1(2),

(d) the outcomes that the carer wishes to achieve in day-to-day life, and

(e) whether, and if so to what extent, the provision of support could contribute to the achievement of those outcomes.

(6) A local authority, in carrying out a carer's assessment, must have regard to—

(a) whether the carer works or wishes to do so, and

(b) whether the carer is participating in or wishes to participate in education, training or recreation.

(7) A local authority, in carrying out a carer's assessment, must involve—

(a) the carer, and

(b) any person whom the carer asks the authority to involve.

(8) When carrying out a carer's assessment, a local authority must also consider—

(a) whether, and if so to what extent, matters other than the provision of support could contribute to the achievement of the outcomes that the carer wishes to achieve in day-to-day life, and

(b) whether the carer would benefit from the provision of anything under section 2 or 4 or of anything which might be available in the community.

(9) An adult is not to be regarded as a carer if the adult provides or intends to provide care—

(a) under or by virtue of a contract, or

(b) as voluntary work.

(10) But in a case where the local authority considers that the relationship between the adult needing care and the adult providing or intending to provide care is such that it would be appropriate for the latter to be regarded as a carer, that adult is to be regarded as such (and subsection (9) is therefore to be ignored in that case).

(11) The references in this section to providing care include a reference to providing practical or emotional support.

(12) This section is subject to section 11(5) to (7) (refusal by carer of assessment).

11 Refusal of assessment

(1) Where an adult refuses a needs assessment, the local authority concerned is not required to carry out the assessment (and section 9(1) does not apply in the adult's case).

(2) But the local authority may not rely on subsection (1) (and so must carry out a needs assessment) if—

(a) the adult lacks capacity to refuse the assessment and the authority is satisfied that carrying out the assessment would be in the adult's best interests, or

(b) the adult is experiencing, or is at risk of, abuse or neglect.

(3) Where, having refused a needs assessment, an adult requests the assessment, section 9(1) applies in the adult's case (and subsection (1) above does not).

(4) Where an adult has refused a needs assessment and the local authority concerned thinks that the adult's needs or circumstances have changed, section 9(1) applies in the adult's case (but subject to further refusal as mentioned in subsection (1) above).

(5) Where a carer refuses a carer's assessment, the local authority concerned is not required to carry out the assessment (and section 10(1) does not apply in the carer's case).

(6) Where, having refused a carer's assessment, a carer requests the assessment, section 10(1) applies in the carer's case (and subsection (5) above does not).

(7) Where a carer has refused a carer's assessment and the local authority concerned thinks that the needs or circumstances of the carer or the adult needing care have changed, section 10(1) applies in the carer's case (but subject to further refusal as mentioned in subsection (5) above).

12 Assessments under sections 9 and 10: further provision

(1) Regulations must make further provision about carrying out a needs or carer's assessment; the regulations may, in particular—

(a) require the local authority, in carrying out the assessment, to have regard to the needs of the family of the adult to whom the assessment relates;

(b) specify other matters to which the local authority must have regard in carrying out the assessment (including, in particular, the matters to which it must have regard in seeking to ensure that the assessment is carried out in an appropriate and proportionate manner);

(c) specify steps that the local authority must take for the purpose of ensuring that the assessment is carried out in an appropriate and proportionate manner;

(d) specify circumstances in which the assessment may or must be carried out by a person (whether or not an officer of the authority) who has expertise in a specified matter or is of such other description as is specified, jointly with or on behalf of the local authority;

(e) specify circumstances in which the adult to whom the assessment relates may carry out the assessment jointly with the local authority;

(f) specify circumstances in which the local authority must, before carrying out the assessment or when doing so, consult a person who has expertise in a specified matter or is of such other description as is specified;

(g) specify circumstances in which the local authority must refer the adult concerned for an assessment of eligibility for NHS continuing healthcare.

(2) The regulations may include provision for facilitating the carrying out of a needs or carer's assessment in circumstances specified under subsection (1)(d) or (e); they may, for example, give the local authority power to provide the person carrying out the assessment—

(a) in the case of a needs assessment, with information about the adult to whom the assessment relates;

(b) in the case of a carer's assessment, with information about the carer to whom the assessment relates and about the adult needing care;

(c) in either case, with whatever resources, or with access to whatever facilities, the authority thinks will be required to carry out the assessment.

(3) The local authority must give a written record of a needs assessment to—

(a) the adult to whom the assessment relates,

(b) any carer that the adult has, if the adult asks the authority to do so, and

(c) any other person to whom the adult asks the authority to give a copy.

(4) The local authority must give a written record of a carer's assessment to—

(a) the carer to whom the assessment relates,

(b) the adult needing care, if the carer asks the authority to do so, and

(c) any other person to whom the carer asks the authority to give a copy.

(5) A local authority may combine a needs or carer's assessment with an assessment it is carrying out (whether or not under this Part) in relation to another person only if the adult to whom the needs or carer's assessment relates agrees and—

(a) where the combination would include an assessment relating to another adult, that other adult agrees;

(b) where the combination would include an assessment relating to a child (including a young carer), the consent condition is met in relation to the child.

(6) The consent condition is met in relation to a child if—

(a) the child has capacity or is competent to agree to the assessments being combined and does so agree, or

(b) the child lacks capacity or is not competent so to agree but the local authority is satisfied that combining the assessments would be in the child's best interests.

(7) Where a local authority is carrying out a needs or carer's assessment, and there is some other assessment being or about to be carried out in relation to the adult to whom the assessment relates or in relation to a relevant person, the local authority may carry out that other assessment—

(a) on behalf of or jointly with the body responsible for carrying it out, or

(b) if that body has arranged to carry out the other assessment jointly with another person, jointly with that body and the other person.

(8) A reference to a needs or carer's assessment includes a reference to a needs or carer's assessment (as the case may be) which forms part of a combined assessment under subsection (5).

(9) A reference to an assessment includes a reference to part of an assessment.

(10) "NHS continuing health care" is to be construed in accordance with standing rules under section 6E of the National Health Service Act 2006.

(11) A person is a "relevant person", in relation to a needs or carer's assessment, if it would be reasonable to combine an assessment relating to that person with the needs or carer's assessment (as mentioned in subsection (5)).

13 The eligibility criteria

(1) Where a local authority is satisfied on the basis of a needs or carer's assessment that an adult has needs for care and support or that a carer has needs for support, it must determine whether any of the needs meet the eligibility criteria (see subsection (7)).

(2) Having made a determination under subsection (1), the local authority must give the adult concerned a written record of the determination and the reasons for it.

(3) Where at least some of an adult's needs for care and support meet the eligibility criteria, the local authority must—

(a) consider what could be done to meet those needs that do,

(b) ascertain whether the adult wants to have those needs met by the local authority in accordance with this Part, and

(c) establish whether the adult is ordinarily resident in the local authority's area.

(4) Where at least some of a carer's needs for support meet the eligibility criteria, the local authority must—

(a) consider what could be done to meet those needs that do, and

(b) establish whether the adult needing care is ordinarily resident in the local authority's area.

(5) Where none of the needs of the adult concerned meet the eligibility criteria, the local authority must give him or her written advice and information about—

(a) what can be done to meet or reduce the needs;

(b) what can be done to prevent or delay the development of needs for care and support, or the development of needs for support, in the future.

(6) Regulations may make provision about the making of the determination under subsection (1).

(7) Needs meet the eligibility criteria if—

(a) they are of a description specified in regulations, or

(b) they form part of a combination of needs of a description so specified.

(8) The regulations may, in particular, describe needs by reference to—

(a) the effect that the needs have on the adult concerned;

(b) the adult's circumstances.

Charging and assessing financial resources

14 Power of local authority to charge

(1) A local authority—

(a) may make a charge for meeting needs under sections 18 to 20, and

(b) where it is meeting needs because Condition 2 in section 18 or Condition 2 or 4 in section 20 is met, may make a charge (in addition to the charge it makes under paragraph (a)) for putting in place the arrangements for meeting those needs.

(2) The power to make a charge under subsection (1) for meeting needs under section 18 is subject to section 15.

(3) The power to make a charge under subsection (1) for meeting a carer's needs for support under section 20 by providing care and support to the adult needing care may not be exercised so as to charge the carer.

(4) A charge under subsection (1)(a) may cover only the cost that the local authority incurs in meeting the needs to which the charge applies.

(5) Regulations may make provision about the exercise of the power to make a charge under subsection (1).

(6) Regulations may prohibit a local authority from making a charge under subsection (1); and the regulations may (in reliance on section 125(7)) prohibit a local authority from doing so where, for example, the care and support or the support—

(a) is of a specified type;
(b) is provided in specified circumstances;
(c) is provided to an adult of a specified description;
(d) is provided for a specified period only.

(7) A local authority may not make a charge under subsection (1) if the income of the adult concerned would, after deduction of the amount of the charge, fall below such amount as is specified in regulations; and the regulations may in particular (in reliance on section 125(7)) specify—

(a) different amounts for different descriptions of care and support;
(b) different amounts for different descriptions of support.

(8) Regulations under subsection (7) may make provision as to cases or circumstances in which an adult is to be treated as having income that would, or as having income that would not, fall below the amount specified in the regulations if a charge were to be made.

15 Cap on care costs

(1) A local authority may not make a charge under section 14 for meeting an adult's needs under section 18 if the total of the costs accrued in meeting the adult's eligible needs after the commencement of this section exceeds the cap on care costs.

(2) The reference to costs accrued in meeting eligible needs is a reference—

(a) in so far as the local authority met those needs, to the cost to the local authority of having done so (as reckoned from the costs specified in the personal budget for meeting those needs (see section 26));
(b) in so far as another local authority met the needs, to the cost to that other local authority of having done so (as reckoned from the costs so specified for meeting those needs);
(c) in so far as a person other than a local authority met the needs, to what the cost of doing so would have been to the local authority which would otherwise

have done so (as reckoned from the costs specified in the independent personal budget for meeting those needs (see section 28).

(3) An adult's needs are "eligible needs" if, at the time they were met—

(a) they met the eligibility criteria,

(b) they were not being met by a carer, and

(c) the adult was ordinarily resident or present in the area of a local authority.

(4) The "cap on care costs" is the amount specified as such in regulations; and the regulations may in particular (in reliance on section 125(7))—

(a) specify different amounts for persons of different age groups;

(b) specify zero as the amount for persons of a specified description.

(5) The total of the costs accrued in meeting an adult's eligible needs after the commencement of this section (as referred to in subsection (1)) is referred to in this Part as the adult's "accrued costs".

(6) Where the costs accrued include daily living costs, the amount attributable to the daily living costs is to be disregarded in working out for the purposes of subsection (1) the total of the costs accrued in meeting an adult's eligible needs after the commencement of this section.

(7) Where the cost to a local authority of meeting an adult's needs under section 18 includes daily living costs, and the accrued costs exceed the cap on care costs (with the result that subsection (1) applies), the local authority may nonetheless make a charge to cover the amount attributable to those daily living costs.

(8) For the purposes of this Part, the amount attributable to an adult's daily living costs is the amount specified in, or determined in accordance with, regulations.

16 Cap on care costs: annual adjustment

(1) Where it appears to the Secretary of State that the level of average earnings in England is different at the end of a review period from what it was at the beginning of that period, the Secretary of State must make regulations under section 15(4) to vary the cap on care costs by the percentage increase or decrease by which that level has changed.

(2) If a variation is made under subsection (1), each adult's accrued costs are to be varied by the same percentage with effect from when the variation itself takes effect (and local authorities must accordingly ensure that care accounts and other records reflect the variation).

(3) The "level of average earnings in England" means the amount which represents the average annual earnings in England estimated in such manner as the Secretary of State thinks fit.

(4) "Review period" means—

(a) the period of 12 months beginning with the day on which section 15 comes into force, and

(b) each subsequent period of 12 months.

(5) The duty under subsection (1) does not restrict the exercise of the power to make regulations under section 15(4).

17 Assessment of financial resources

(1) Where a local authority, having made a determination under section 13(1), thinks that, if it were to meet an adult's needs for care and support, it would charge the adult under section 14(1) for meeting at least some of the needs, it must assess—

(a) the level of the adult's financial resources, and

(b) the amount (if any) which the adult would be likely to be able to pay towards the cost of meeting the needs for care and support.

(2) Where a local authority thinks that, in meeting an adult's needs for care and support, it would make a charge under section 15(7), it must assess—

(a) the level of the adult's financial resources, and

(b) the amount (if any) which the adult would be likely to be able to pay towards the amount attributable to the adult's daily living costs.

(3) Where a local authority, having made a determination under section 13(1), thinks that, if it were to meet a carer's needs for support, it would charge the carer under section 14(1) for meeting at least some of the needs, it must assess—

(a) the level of the carer's financial resources, and

(b) the amount (if any) which the carer would be likely to be able to pay towards the cost of meeting the needs for support.

(4) Where a local authority, having made a determination under section 13(1), thinks that, if it were to meet a carer's needs for support, it would charge the adult needing care under section 14(1) for meeting at least some of the needs, it must assess—

(a) the level of the financial resources of the adult needing care, and

(b) the amount (if any) which the adult needing care would be likely to be able to pay towards the cost of meeting the carer's needs for support.

(5) An assessment under this section is referred to in this Part as a "financial assessment".

(6) A local authority, having carried out a financial assessment, must give a written record of the assessment to the adult to whom it relates.

(7) Regulations must make provision about the carrying out of a financial assessment.

(8) The regulations must make provision as to cases or circumstances in which, if the financial resources of an adult who has needs for care and support (whether in terms of income, capital or a combination of both) exceed a specified level, a local authority is not permitted to, or may (but need not)—

(a) in a case where the adult's accrued costs do not exceed the cap on care costs, pay towards the cost of the provision of care and support for the adult;

(b) in a case where the adult's accrued costs exceed the cap on care costs, pay towards the amount attributable to the adult's daily living costs.

(9) The regulations must make provision as to cases or circumstances in which, if the financial resources of a carer who has needs for support or of the adult needing care (whether in terms of income, capital or a combination of both) exceed a specified level, a local authority is not permitted to, or may (but need not), pay towards the cost of the provision of support for the carer.

(10) The level specified for the purposes of subsections (8) and (9) is referred to in this Part as "the financial limit"; and the regulations may in particular (in reliance on section 125(7)) specify—

(a) different levels for different descriptions of care and support;
(b) different levels for different descriptions of support.

(11) The regulations must make provision for—
(a) calculating income;
(b) calculating capital.

(12) The regulations may make provision—
(a) for treating, or not treating, amounts of a specified type as income or as capital;
(b) as to cases or circumstances in which an adult is to be treated as having, or as not having, financial resources above the financial limit.

(13) The regulations may make provision as to cases or circumstances in which a local authority is to be treated as—
(a) having carried out a financial assessment in an adult's case, and
(b) being satisfied on that basis that the adult's financial resources exceed, or that they do not exceed, the financial limit.

Duties and powers to meet needs

18 Duty to meet needs for care and support

(1) A local authority, having made a determination under section 13(1), must meet the adult's needs for care and support which meet the eligibility criteria if—
(a) the adult is ordinarily resident in the authority's area or is present in its area but of no settled residence,
(b) the adult's accrued costs do not exceed the cap on care costs, and
(c) there is no charge under section 14 for meeting the needs or, in so far as there is, condition 1, 2 or 3 is met.

(2) Condition 1 is met if the local authority is satisfied on the basis of the financial assessment it carried out that the adult's financial resources are at or below the financial limit.

(3) Condition 2 is met if—
(a) the local authority is satisfied on the basis of the financial assessment it carried out that the adult's financial resources are above the financial limit, but
(b) the adult nonetheless asks the authority to meet the adult's needs.

(4) Condition 3 is met if—
(a) the adult lacks capacity to arrange for the provision of care and support, but
(b) there is no person authorised to do so under the Mental Capacity Act 2005 or otherwise in a position to do so on the adult's behalf.

(5) A local authority, having made a determination under section 13(1), must meet the adult's needs for care and support which meet the eligibility criteria if—
(a) the adult is ordinarily resident in the authority's area or is present in its area but of no settled residence, and
(b) the adult's accrued costs exceed the cap on care costs.

(6) The reference in subsection (1) to there being no charge under section 14 for meeting an adult's needs for care and support is a reference to there being no such charge because—

(a) the authority is prohibited by regulations under section 14 from making such a charge, or

(b) the authority is entitled to make such a charge but decides not to do so.

(7) The duties under subsections (1) and (5) do not apply to such of the adult's needs as are being met by a carer.

19 Power to meet needs for care and support

(1) A local authority, having carried out a needs assessment and (if required to do so) a financial assessment, may meet an adult's needs for care and support if—

(a) the adult is ordinarily resident in the authority's area or is present in its area but of no settled residence, and

(b) the authority is satisfied that it is not required to meet the adult's needs under section 18.

(2) A local authority, having made a determination under section 13(1), may meet an adult's needs for care and support which meet the eligibility criteria if—

(a) the adult is ordinarily resident in the area of another local authority,

(b) there is no charge under section 14 for meeting the needs or, in so far as there is such a charge, condition 1, 2 or 3 in section 18 is met, and

(c) the authority has notified the other local authority of its intention to meet the needs.

(3) A local authority may meet an adult's needs for care and support which appear to it to be urgent (regardless of whether the adult is ordinarily resident in its area) without having yet—

(a) carried out a needs assessment or a financial assessment, or

(b) made a determination under section 13(1).

(4) A local authority may meet an adult's needs under subsection (3) where, for example, the adult is terminally ill (within the meaning given in section 82(4) of the Welfare Reform Act 2012).

(5) The reference in subsection (2) to there being no charge under section 14 for meeting an adult's needs is to be construed in accordance with section 18(6).

20 Duty and power to meet a carer's needs for support

(1) A local authority, having made a determination under section 13(1), must meet a carer's needs for support which meet the eligibility criteria if—

(a) the adult needing care is ordinarily resident in the local authority's area or is present in its area but of no settled residence,

(b) in so far as meeting the carer's needs involves the provision of support to the carer, there is no charge under section 14 for meeting the needs or, in so far as there is, condition 1 or 2 is met, and

(c) in so far as meeting the carer's needs involves the provision of care and support to the adult needing care—

(i) there is no charge under section 14 for meeting the needs and the adult needing care agrees to the needs being met in that way, or

(ii) in so far as there is such a charge, condition 3 or 4 is met.

(2) Condition 1 is met if the local authority is satisfied on the basis of the financial assessment it carried out that the carer's financial resources are at or below the financial limit.

(3) Condition 2 is met if—

(a) the local authority is satisfied on the basis of the financial assessment it carried out that the carer's financial resources are above the financial limit, but

(b) the carer nonetheless asks the authority to meet the needs in question.

(4) Condition 3 is met if—

(a) the local authority is satisfied on the basis of the financial assessment it carried out that the financial resources of the adult needing care are at or below the financial limit, and

(b) the adult needing care agrees to the authority meeting the needs in question by providing care and support to him or her.

(5) Condition 4 is met if—

(a) the local authority is satisfied on the basis of the financial assessment it carried out that the financial resources of the adult needing care are above the financial limit, but

(b) the adult needing care nonetheless asks the authority to meet the needs in question by providing care and support to him or her.

(6) A local authority may meet a carer's needs for support if it is satisfied that it is not required to meet the carer's needs under this section; but, in so far as meeting the carer's needs involves the provision of care and support to the adult needing care, it may do so only if the adult needing care agrees to the needs being met in that way.

(7) A local authority may meet some or all of a carer's needs for support in a way which involves the provision of care and support to the adult needing care, even if the authority would not be required to meet the adult's needs for care and support under section 18.

(8) Where a local authority is required by this section to meet some or all of a carer's needs for support but it does not prove feasible for it to do so by providing care and support to the adult needing care, it must, so far as it is feasible to do so, identify some other way in which to do so.

(9) The reference in subsection (1)(b) to there being no charge under section 14 for meeting a carer's needs for support is a reference to there being no such charge because—

(a) the authority is prohibited by regulations under section 14 from making such a charge, or

(b) the authority is entitled to make such a charge but decides not to do so.

(10) The reference in subsection (1)(c) to there being no charge under section 14 for meeting an adult's needs for care and support is to be construed in accordance with section 18(6).

21 Exception for persons subject to immigration control

(1) A local authority may not meet the needs for care and support of an adult to whom section 115 of the Immigration and Asylum Act 1999 ("the 1999 Act") (exclusion from benefits) applies and whose needs for care and support have arisen solely—

(a) because the adult is destitute, or

(b) because of the physical effects, or anticipated physical effects, of being destitute.

(2) For the purposes of subsection (1), section 95(2) to (7) of the 1999 Act applies but with the references in section 95(4) and (5) to the Secretary of State being read as references to the local authority in question.

(3) But, until the commencement of section 44(6) of the Nationality, Immigration and Asylum Act 2002, subsection (2) is to have effect as if it read as follows—

"(2) For the purposes of subsection (1), section 95(3) and (5) to (8) of, and paragraph 2 of Schedule 8 to, the 1999 Act apply but with references in section 95(5) and (7) and that paragraph to the Secretary of State being read as references to the local authority in question."

(4) The reference in subsection (1) to meeting an adult's needs for care and support includes a reference to providing care and support to the adult in order to meet a carer's needs for support.

(5) For the purposes of its application in relation to the duty in section 2(1) (preventing needs for care and support), this section is to be read as if—

(a) for subsection (1) there were substituted—

"(1) A local authority may not perform the duty under section 2(1) in relation to an adult to whom section 115 of the Immigration and Asylum Act 1999 ("the 1999 Act") (exclusion from benefits) applies and whose needs for care and support have arisen, or for whom such needs may in the future arise, solely—

(a) because the adult is destitute, or

(b) because of the physical effects, or anticipated physical effects, of being destitute.", and

(b) subsection (4) were omitted.

22 Exception for provision of health services

(1) A local authority may not meet needs under sections 18 to 20 by providing or arranging for the provision of a service or facility that is required to be provided under the National Health Service Act 2006 unless—

(a) doing so would be merely incidental or ancillary to doing something else to meet needs under those sections, and

(b) the service or facility in question would be of a nature that the local authority could be expected to provide.

(2) Regulations may specify—

(a) types of services or facilities which, despite subsection (1), may be provided or the provision of which may be arranged by a local authority, or circumstances in which such services or facilities may be so provided or the provision of which may be so arranged;

(b) types of services or facilities which may not be provided or the provision of which may not be arranged by a local authority, or circumstances in which such services or facilities may not be so provided or the provision of which may not be so arranged;

(c) services or facilities, or a method for determining services or facilities, the provision of which is, or is not, to be treated as meeting the conditions in subsection (1)(a) and (b).

(3) A local authority may not meet needs under sections 18 to 20 by providing or arranging for the provision of nursing care by a registered nurse.

(4) But a local authority may, despite the prohibitions in subsections (1) and (3), arrange for the provision of accommodation together with the provision of nursing care by a registered nurse if—

(a) the authority has obtained consent for it to arrange for the provision of the nursing care from whichever clinical commissioning group regulations require, or

(b) the case is urgent and the arrangements for accommodation are only temporary.

(5) In a case to which subsection (4)(b) applies, as soon as is feasible after the temporary arrangements are made, the local authority must seek to obtain the consent mentioned in subsection (4)(a).

(6) Regulations may require a local authority—

(a) to be involved in the specified manner in processes for assessing a person's needs for health care and for deciding how those needs should be met;

(b) to make arrangements for determining disputes between the authority and a clinical commissioning group or the National Health Service Commissioning Board about whether or not a service or facility is required to be provided under the National Health Service Act 2006.

(7) Nothing in this section affects what a local authority may do under the National Health Service Act 2006, including entering into arrangements under regulations under section 75 of that Act (arrangements with NHS bodies).

(8) A reference to the provision of nursing care by a registered nurse is a reference to the provision by a registered nurse of a service involving—

(a) the provision of care, or

(b) the planning, supervision or delegation of the provision of care,

other than a service which, having regard to its nature and the circumstances in which it is provided, does not need to be provided by a registered nurse.

(9) Where, in a case within subsection (4), the National Health Service Commissioning Board has responsibility for arranging for the provision of the nursing care, the reference in paragraph (a) of that subsection to a clinical commissioning group is to be read as a reference to the Board.

(10) For the purposes of its application in relation to the duty in section 2(1) (preventing needs for care and support), this section is to be read as if references to meeting needs under sections 18 to 20 were references to performing the duty under section 2(1).

23 Exception for provision of housing etc.

(1) A local authority may not meet needs under sections 18 to 20 by doing anything which it or another local authority is required to do under—

(a) the Housing Act 1996, or

(b) any other enactment specified in regulations.

(2) "Another local authority" includes a district council for an area in England for which there is also a county council.

(3) For the purposes of its application in relation to the duty in section 2(1) (preventing needs for care and support), this section is to be read as if, in subsection (1), for "meet needs under sections 18 to 20" there were substituted "perform the duty under section 2(1)".

Next steps after assessments

24 The steps for the local authority to take

(1) Where a local authority is required to meet needs under section 18 or 20(1), or decides to do so under section 19(1) or (2) or 20(6), it must—

(a) prepare a care and support plan or a support plan for the adult concerned,

(b) tell the adult which (if any) of the needs that it is going to meet may be met by direct payments, and

(c) help the adult with deciding how to have the needs met.

(2) Where a local authority has carried out a needs or carer's assessment but is not required to meet needs under section 18 or 20(1), and does not decide to do so under section 19(1) or (2) or 20(6), it must give the adult concerned—

(a) its written reasons for not meeting the needs, and

(b) (unless it has already done so under section 13(5)) advice and information about—

(i) what can be done to meet or reduce the needs;

(ii) what can be done to prevent or delay the development by the adult concerned of needs for care and support or of needs for support in the future.

(3) Where a local authority is not going to meet an adult's needs for care and support, it must nonetheless prepare an independent personal budget for the adult (see section 28) if—

(a) the needs meet the eligibility criteria,

(b) at least some of the needs are not being met by a carer, and

(c) the adult is ordinarily resident in the authority's area or is present in its area but of no settled residence.

25 Care and support plan, support plan

(1) A care and support plan or, in the case of a carer, a support plan is a document prepared by a local authority which—

(a) specifies the needs identified by the needs assessment or carer's assessment,

(b) specifies whether, and if so to what extent, the needs meet the eligibility criteria,
(c) specifies the needs that the local authority is going to meet and how it is going to meet them,
(d) specifies to which of the matters referred to in section 9(4) the provision of care and support could be relevant or to which of the matters referred to in section 10(5) and (6) the provision of support could be relevant,
(e) includes the personal budget for the adult concerned (see section 26), and
(f) includes advice and information about—
(i) what can be done to meet or reduce the needs in question;
(ii) what can be done to prevent or delay the development of needs for care and support or of needs for support in the future.

(2) Where some or all of the needs are to be met by making direct payments, the plan must also specify—
(a) the needs which are to be so met, and
(b) the amount and frequency of the direct payments.

(3) In preparing a care and support plan, the local authority must involve—
(a) the adult for whom it is being prepared,
(b) any carer that the adult has, and
(c) any person whom the adult asks the authority to involve or, where the adult lacks capacity to ask the authority to do that, any person who appears to the authority to be interested in the adult's welfare.

(4) In preparing a support plan, the local authority must involve—
(a) the carer for whom it is being prepared,
(b) the adult needing care, if the carer asks the authority to do so, and
(c) any other person whom the carer asks the authority to involve.

(5) In performing the duty under subsection (3)(a) or (4)(a), the local authority must take all reasonable steps to reach agreement with the adult or carer for whom the plan is being prepared about how the authority should meet the needs in question.

(6) In seeking to ensure that the plan is proportionate to the needs to be met, the local authority must have regard in particular—
(a) in the case of a care and support plan, to the matters referred to in section 9(4);
(b) in the case of a support plan, to the matters referred to in section 10(5) and (6).

(7) The local authority may authorise a person (including the person for whom the plan is to be prepared) to prepare the plan jointly with the authority.

(8) The local authority may do things to facilitate the preparation of the plan in a case within subsection (7); it may, for example, provide a person authorised under that subsection with—
(a) in the case of a care and support plan, information about the adult for whom the plan is being prepared;
(b) in the case of a support plan, information about the carer and the adult needing care;
(c) in either case, whatever resources, or access to whatever facilities, the authority thinks are required to prepare the plan.

(9) The local authority must give a copy of a care and support plan to—
(a) the adult for whom it has been prepared,
(b) any carer that the adult has, if the adult asks the authority to do so, and
(c) any other person to whom the adult asks the authority to give a copy.

(10) The local authority must give a copy of a support plan to—
(a) the carer for whom it has been prepared,
(b) the adult needing care, if the carer asks the authority to do so, and
(c) any other person to whom the carer asks the authority to give a copy.

(11) A local authority may combine a care and support plan or a support plan with a plan (whether or not prepared by it and whether or not under this Part) relating to another person only if the adult for whom the care and support plan or the support plan is being prepared agrees and—
(a) where the combination would include a plan prepared for another adult, that other adult agrees;
(b) where the combination would include a plan prepared for a child (including a young carer), the consent condition is met in relation to the child.

(12) The consent condition is met in relation to a child if—
(a) the child has capacity or is competent to agree to the plans being combined and does so agree, or
(b) the child lacks capacity or is not competent so to agree but the local authority is satisfied that the combining the plans would be in the child's best interests.

(13) Regulations may specify cases or circumstances in which such of paragraphs (a) to (f) of subsection (1) and paragraphs (a) and (b) of subsection (2) as are specified do not apply.

(14) The regulations may in particular specify that the paragraphs in question do not apply as regards specified needs or matters.

26 Personal budget

(1) A personal budget for an adult is a statement which specifies—
(a) the cost to the local authority of meeting those of the adult's needs which it is required or decides to meet as mentioned in section 24(1),
(b) the amount which, on the basis of the financial assessment, the adult must pay towards that cost, and
(c) if on that basis the local authority must itself pay towards that cost, the amount which it must pay.

(2) In the case of an adult with needs for care and support which the local authority is required to meet under section 18, the personal budget must also specify—
(a) the cost to the local authority of meeting the adult's needs under that section, and
(b) where that cost includes daily living costs—
(i) the amount attributable to those daily living costs, and
(ii) the balance of the cost referred to in paragraph (a).

(3) A personal budget for an adult may also specify other amounts of public money that are available in the adult's case including, for example, amounts available for spending on matters relating to housing, health care or welfare.

(4) Regulations may make provision for excluding costs to a local authority from a personal budget if the costs are incurred in meeting needs for which the authority—

(a) does not make a charge, or

(b) is not permitted to make a charge.

27 Review of care and support plan or of support plan

(1) A local authority must—

(a) keep under review generally care and support plans, and support plans, that it has prepared, and

(b) on a reasonable request by or on behalf of the adult to whom a care and support plan relates or the carer to whom a support plan relates, review the plan.

(2) A local authority may revise a care and support plan; and in deciding whether or how to do so, it—

(a) must have regard in particular to the matters referred to in section 9(4) (and specified in the plan under section 25(1)(d)), and

(b) must involve—

(i) the adult to whom the plan relates,

(ii) any carer that the adult has, and

(iii) any person whom the adult asks the authority to involve or, where the adult lacks capacity to ask the authority to do that, any person who appears to the authority to be interested in the adult's welfare.

(3) A local authority may revise a support plan; and in deciding whether or how to do so, it—

(a) must have regard in particular to the matters referred to in section 10(5) and (6) (and specified in the plan under section 25(1)(d)), and

(b) must involve—

(i) the carer to whom the plan relates,

(ii) the adult needing care, if the carer asks the authority to do so, and

(iii) any other person whom the carer asks the authority to involve.

(4) Where a local authority is satisfied that circumstances have changed in a way that affects a care and support plan or a support plan, the authority must—

(a) to the extent it thinks appropriate, carry out a needs or carer's assessment, carry out a financial assessment and make a determination under section 13(1), and

(b) revise the care and support plan or support plan accordingly.

(5) Where, in a case within subsection (4), the local authority is proposing to change how it meets the needs in question, it must, in performing the duty under subsection (2)(b)(i) or (3)(b)(i), take all reasonable steps to reach agreement with the adult concerned about how it should meet those needs.

28 Independent personal budget

(1) An independent personal budget is a statement which specifies what the cost would be to the local authority concerned (see section 24(3)) of meeting the adult's eligible needs for care and support.

(2) Where the amount referred to in subsection (1) includes daily living costs, the independent personal budget for the adult must specify—

(a) the amount attributable to those daily living costs, and

(b) the balance of the amount referred to in subsection (1).

(3) An adult's needs are "eligible needs" if, at the time they were met—

(a) they met the eligibility criteria,

(b) they were not being met by a carer, and

(c) the adult was ordinarily resident or present in the area of the local authority.

(4) A local authority must—

(a) keep under review generally independent personal budgets that it has prepared, and

(b) on a reasonable request by or on behalf of the adult to whom an independent personal budget relates, review the independent personal budget.

(5) A local authority may revise an independent personal budget; and in deciding whether or how to do so, it must, in so far as it is feasible to do so, involve—

(a) the adult to whom the independent personal budget relates,

(b) any carer that the adult has, and

(c) any other person whom the adult asks the authority to involve or, where the adult lacks capacity to ask the authority to do that, any person who appears to the authority to be interested in the adult's welfare.

(6) Where a local authority is satisfied that the circumstances of the adult to whom an independent personal budget applies have changed in a way that affects the independent personal budget, the authority must—

(a) to the extent it thinks appropriate, carry out a needs assessment and make a determination under section 13(1), and

(b) revise the independent personal budget accordingly.

(7) Where, in a case within subsection (6), an adult refuses a needs assessment and the local authority thinks that the adult's refusal is unreasonable, it need no longer keep an up-to-date care account in the adult's case.

(8) Having reviewed an independent personal budget, a local authority must—

(a) if it revises the independent personal budget, notify the adult to whom the independent personal budget relates of the revisions and provide an explanation of the effect of each revision, or

(b) if it does not revise the independent personal budget, notify the adult accordingly.

29 Care account

(1) Where an adult has needs for care and support which meet the eligibility criteria, the local authority in whose area the adult is ordinarily resident or, if the adult is of no settled residence, in whose area the adult is present—

(a) must keep an up-to-date record of the adult's accrued costs (a "care account"), and
(b) once those costs exceed the cap on care costs, must inform the adult.

(2) Where a local authority which has been keeping a care account is no longer required to do so, it must nonetheless retain the account that it has kept so far until—
(a) the end of the period of 99 years beginning with the day on which it last updated the account, or
(b) where the adult dies, the local authority becomes aware of the death.

(3) A care account must specify such amount as is attributable to the adult's daily living costs.

(4) A local authority which is keeping a care account must, at such times as regulations may specify, provide the adult concerned with a statement which—
(a) sets out the adult's accrued costs, and
(b) includes such other matters as regulations may specify.

(5) Regulations may specify circumstances in which the duty under subsection (4) does not apply.

30 Cases where adult expresses preference for particular accommodation

(1) Regulations may provide that where—
(a) a local authority is going to meet needs under sections 18 to 20 by providing or arranging for the provision of accommodation of a specified type,
(b) the adult for whom the accommodation is going to be provided expresses a preference for particular accommodation of that type, and
(c) specified conditions are met,

the local authority must provide or arrange for the provision of the preferred accommodation.

(2) The regulations may provide for the adult or a person of a specified description to pay for some or all of the additional cost in specified cases or circumstances.

(3) "Additional cost" means the cost of providing or arranging for the provision of the preferred accommodation less that part of the amount specified in the personal budget for the purposes of section 26(1)(a) that relates to the provision of accommodation of that type.

Direct payments

31 Adults with capacity to request direct payments

(1) This section applies where—
(a) a personal budget for an adult specifies an amount which the local authority must pay towards the cost of meeting the needs to which the personal budget relates, and
(b) the adult requests the local authority to meet some or all of those needs by making payments to the adult or a person nominated by the adult.

(2) If conditions 1 to 4 are met, the local authority must, subject to regulations under section 33, make the payments to which the request relates to the adult or nominated person.

(3) A payment under this section is referred to in this Part as a "direct payment".

(4) Condition 1 is that—

(a) the adult has capacity to make the request, and

(b) where there is a nominated person, that person agrees to receive the payments.

(5) Condition 2 is that—

(a) the local authority is not prohibited by regulations under section 33 from meeting the adult's needs by making direct payments to the adult or nominated person, and

(b) if regulations under that section give the local authority discretion to decide not to meet the adult's needs by making direct payments to the adult or nominated person, it does not exercise that discretion.

(6) Condition 3 is that the local authority is satisfied that the adult or nominated person is capable of managing direct payments—

(a) by himself or herself, or

(b) with whatever help the authority thinks the adult or nominated person will be able to access.

(7) Condition 4 is that the local authority is satisfied that making direct payments to the adult or nominated person is an appropriate way to meet the needs in question.

32 Adults without capacity to request direct payments

(1) This section applies where—

(a) a personal budget for an adult specifies an amount which the local authority must pay towards the cost of meeting the needs to which the personal budget relates, and

(b) the adult lacks capacity to request the local authority to meet any of those needs by making payments to the adult, but

(c) an authorised person requests the local authority to meet some or all of those needs by making payments to the authorised person.

(2) If conditions 1 to 5 are met, the local authority must, subject to regulations under section 33, make the payments to which the request relates to the authorised person.

(3) A payment under this section is referred to in this Part as a "direct payment".

(4) A person is authorised for the purposes of this section if—

(a) the person is authorised under the Mental Capacity Act 2005 to make decisions about the adult's needs for care and support,

(b) where the person is not authorised as mentioned in paragraph (a), a person who is so authorised agrees with the local authority that the person is a suitable person to whom to make direct payments, or

(c) where the person is not authorised as mentioned in paragraph (a) and there is no person who is so authorised, the local authority considers that the person is a suitable person to whom to make direct payments.

(5) Condition 1 is that, where the authorised person is not authorised as mentioned in subsection (4)(a) but there is at least one person who is so authorised, a person who is so authorised supports the authorised person's request.

(6) Condition 2 is that—

(a) the local authority is not prohibited by regulations under section 33 from meeting the adult's needs by making direct payments to the authorised person, and

(b) if regulations under that section give the local authority discretion to decide not to meet the adult's needs by making direct payments to the authorised person, it does not exercise that discretion.

(7) Condition 3 is that the local authority is satisfied that the authorised person will act in the adult's best interests in arranging for the provision of the care and support for which the direct payments under this section would be used.

(8) Condition 4 is that the local authority is satisfied that the authorised person is capable of managing direct payments—

(a) by himself or herself, or

(b) with whatever help the authority thinks the authorised person will be able to access.

(9) Condition 5 is that the local authority is satisfied that making direct payments to the authorised person is an appropriate way to meet the needs in question.

33 Direct payments: further provision

(1) Regulations must make further provision about direct payments.

(2) The regulations may, in particular, specify—

(a) cases or circumstances in which a local authority must not, or cases or circumstances in which it has the discretion to decide not to, meet needs by making direct payments;

(b) conditions which a local authority may or must attach to the making of direct payments;

(c) matters to which a local authority may or must have regard when making a decision of a specified type in relation to direct payments;

(d) steps which a local authority may or must take before, or after, making a decision of a specified type in relation to direct payments;

(e) cases or circumstances in which an adult who lacks capacity to request the making of direct payments must or may nonetheless be regarded for the purposes of this Part or the regulations as having capacity to do so;

(f) cases or circumstances in which an adult who no longer lacks capacity to make such a request must or may nonetheless be regarded for any of those purposes as lacking capacity to do so;

(g) cases or circumstances in which a local authority making direct payments must review the making of those payments.

(3) A direct payment is made on condition that it be used only to pay for arrangements under which the needs specified under section 25(2)(a) in the care and support plan or (as the case may be) the support plan are met.

(4) In a case where one or more of conditions 1 to 4 in section 31 is no longer met or one or more of conditions 1 to 5 in section 32 is no longer met, the local authority must terminate the making of direct payments.

(5) In a case where a condition specified under subsection (2)(b) or the condition mentioned in subsection (3) is breached, the local authority—

(a) may terminate the making of direct payments, and

(b) may require repayment of the whole or part of a direct payment (with section 69 accordingly applying to sums which the local authority requires to be repaid).

Deferred payment agreements, etc.

34 Deferred payment agreements and loans

(1) Regulations may, in such cases or circumstances and subject to such conditions as may be specified, require or permit a local authority to enter into a deferred payment agreement with an adult.

(2) A "deferred payment agreement" is an agreement under which a local authority agrees not to require until the specified time either or both of the following—

(a) the payment of the specified part of the amounts due from an adult to the authority under such provision of this Part or of regulations under this Part as is specified in regulations;

(b) the repayment of the specified part of a loan made under the agreement by the authority to an adult for the purpose of assisting the adult to obtain the provision of care and support for the adult.

(3) The care and support mentioned in subsection (2)(b) includes care and support the provision of which—

(a) the authority does not consider to be necessary to meet the adult's needs;

(b) is in addition to care and support which is being provided, arranged for, or paid for (in whole or in part) by the authority.

(4) Regulations under subsection (1) may, in particular, prohibit a local authority from entering into, or permit it to refuse to enter into, a deferred payment agreement unless it obtains adequate security for the payment of the adult's deferred amount.

(5) Regulations may specify what constitutes adequate security for the purposes of subsection (4); they may, for example, specify—

(a) an obligation on the adult to give the authority a charge over the adult's legal or beneficial interest in the property which the adult occupies as his or her only or main residence (or in a property which the adult used to occupy as such) to secure payment of the adult's deferred amount;

(b) a guarantee from another person to pay the adult's deferred amount.

(6) A reference in this section or section 35 to an adult's deferred amount, in relation to a deferred payment agreement, is a reference to the amount of which the local authority agrees not to require payment or repayment until the specified time.

(7) "Specified", in relation to a time or a part of an amount or loan, means specified in or determined in accordance with regulations; and the specified part of an amount or loan may be 100%.

(8) This section applies in relation to an agreement under which a local authority agrees to make a loan to an adult for the purpose of assisting the adult to obtain the provision of care and support for the adult as it applies in relation to a deferred payment agreement; and for that purpose—

(a) the reference in subsection (3) to subsection (2)(b) is to be read as a reference to this subsection; and

(b) the references in subsections (4) and (5) to payment of the adult's deferred amount are to be read as references to repayment of the loan.

35 Deferred payment agreements and loans: further provision

(1) Regulations may require or permit a local authority to charge—

(a) interest on an adult's deferred amount;

(b) such amount relating to the authority's administrative costs as is specified in or determined in accordance with the regulations;

(c) interest on an amount charged under paragraph (b).

(2) The regulations may specify costs which are, or which are not, to be regarded as administrative costs for the purposes of subsection (1)(b).

(3) The regulations may—

(a) require or permit adequate security to be obtained for the payment of any interest or other amount referred to in subsection (1);

(b) require or permit any such interest or other amount to be treated in the same way as the adult's deferred amount;

(c) specify what constitutes adequate security for the purposes of paragraph (a).

(4) The authority may not charge interest under regulations made under subsection (1) or under a deferred payment agreement at a rate that exceeds the rate specified in or determined in accordance with the regulations; the regulations may, for example, provide for a rate to be determined by reference to a specified interest rate or other specified criterion.

(5) The regulations must enable the adult to terminate a deferred payment agreement by—

(a) giving the authority notice, and

(b) paying the authority the full amount for which the adult is liable with respect to the adult's deferred amount and any interest or other amount charged under regulations made under subsection (1) or under the agreement.

(6) The regulations may make other provision about the duration of a deferred payment agreement and for its termination by either party.

(7) The regulations may make provision as to the rights and obligations of the authority and the adult where the adult disposes of any legal or beneficial interest in a property to which a deferred payment agreement relates and acquires a legal or beneficial interest in another property (whether or not it is in the area of that authority); they may, for example, make provision—

(a) for the authority not to require payment of the amounts referred to in subsection (5)(b) until the time specified in or determined in accordance with the regulations;

(b) for the adult to give the authority a charge over the adult's legal or beneficial interest in the other property.

(8) The regulations may—

(a) require or permit terms or conditions of a specified description, or in a specified form, to be included in a deferred payment agreement;

(b) permit such other terms or conditions as the authority considers appropriate to be included in such an agreement;

(c) require statements or other information relating to specified matters, or in a specified form, to be included in such an agreement.

(9) The regulations may make provision for the purpose of enabling local authorities to protect (for example, by registration) or enforce security obtained for the payment of the adult's deferred amount or the payment of any interest or other amount referred to in subsection (1); and, for that purpose, the regulations may amend, repeal, or revoke an enactment, or provide for an enactment to apply with specified modifications.

(10) This section applies in relation to an agreement of the kind mentioned in section 34(8) as it applies in relation to a deferred payment agreement; and for that purpose—

(a) the references in subsections (1), (3) and (5) to the adult's deferred amount are to be read as references to the loan; and

(b) the reference in subsection (9) to payment of the adult's deferred amount is to be read as a reference to repayment of the loan.

36 Alternative financial arrangements

(1) Regulations may, in such cases or circumstances and subject to such conditions as may be specified, require or permit a local authority to enter into alternative financial arrangements of a specified description with an adult.

(2) "Alternative financial arrangements" means arrangements which in the Secretary of State's opinion—

(a) equate in substance to a deferred payment agreement or an agreement of the kind mentioned in section 34(8), but

(b) achieve a similar effect to an agreement of the kind in question without including provision for the payment of interest.

(3) The regulations may make provision in connection with alternative financial arrangements to which they apply, including, in particular, provision of the kind that may (or must) be made in regulations under section 34 or 35 (apart from provision for the payment of interest).

Continuity of care and support when adult moves

37 Notification, assessment, etc.

(1) This section applies where—

(a) an adult's needs for care and support are being met by a local authority ("the first authority") under section 18 or 19,

(b) the adult notifies another local authority ("the second authority") (or that authority is notified on the adult's behalf) that the adult intends to move to the area of the second authority, and

(c) the second authority is satisfied that the adult's intention is genuine.

(2) This section also applies where—

(a) an adult is not having needs for care and support met under either of those sections but a local authority ("the first authority") is nonetheless keeping a care account in the adult's case,

(b) the adult notifies another local authority ("the second authority") (or that authority is notified on the adult's behalf) that the adult intends to move to the area of the second authority, and

(c) the second authority is satisfied that the adult's intention is genuine.

(3) This section also applies where—

(a) an adult's needs for care and support are being met by a local authority ("the first authority") under section 18 or 19 by the first authority arranging for the provision of accommodation in the area of another local authority ("the second authority"),

(b) the adult notifies the second authority (or that authority is notified on the adult's behalf) that the adult intends to move out of that accommodation but to remain, and be provided with care and support at home or in the community, in its area, and

(c) the second authority is satisfied that the adult's intention is genuine.

(4) The second authority must—

(a) provide the adult and, if the adult has or is proposing to have a carer, the carer with such information as it considers appropriate (in so far as it would not do so under section 4), and

(b) notify the first authority that it is satisfied as mentioned in subsection (1)(c), (2)(c) or (3)(c).

(5) The first authority, having received the notification under subsection (4)(b), must provide the second authority with—

(a) a copy of any care and support plan prepared for the adult,

(b) a copy of any independent personal budget prepared for the adult,

(c) in a case within subsection (2), a copy of the most recent needs assessment in the adult's case,

(d) if the first authority has been keeping a care account in the adult's case, a copy of that account,

(e) if the adult has a carer and that carer is to continue as the adult's carer after the move, a copy of any support plan prepared for the carer, and

(f) such other information relating to the adult and, if the adult has a carer (whether or not one with needs for support), such other information relating to the carer as the second authority may request.

(6) The second authority must—

(a) assess whether the adult has needs for care and support and, if the adult does, what those needs are, and

(b) where the adult has or is proposing to have a carer and it is appropriate to do so, assess whether the carer has or is likely to have needs for support and, if the carer does or is likely to, what those needs are or are likely to be.

(7) In carrying out an assessment under subsection (6)(a) or (b), the second authority must have regard to the care and support plan provided under subsection (5)(a) or (as the case may be) the support plan provided under subsection (5)(e).

(8) This Part—

(a) applies to an assessment under subsection (6)(a) as it applies to a needs assessment, and

(b) applies to an assessment under subsection (6)(b) as it applies to a carer's assessment.

(9) Pending the adult's move, the first authority must keep in contact with the second authority in order to ascertain the progress that the second authority is making in preparing to meet—

(a) any needs for care and support under section 18 or 19 in the adult's case, and

(b) where the adult is proposing to have a carer immediately after the move, any needs for support under section 20 in the carer's case.

(10) The first authority must keep the adult (and, where applicable, the carer) informed about its contact under subsection (9) with the second authority and must involve the adult (and, where applicable, the carer) in the contact.

(11) Where the needs identified by an assessment under subsection (6)(a) carried out by the second authority are different from those specified in the care and support plan provided under subsection (5)(a), the second authority must provide a written explanation of the difference to—

(a) the adult,

(b) any carer that the adult has, if the adult asks the authority to do so, and

(c) any other person to whom the adult asks the authority to provide the explanation.

(12) Where the cost to the second authority of meeting the adult's eligible needs is different from the cost to the first authority of doing so, the second authority must provide a written explanation of the difference to—

(a) the adult,

(b) any carer that the adult has, if the adult asks the authority to do so, and

(c) any other person to whom the adult asks the authority to provide the explanation.

(13) Where the needs identified by an assessment under subsection (6)(b) carried out by the second authority are different from those in the support plan provided under subsection (5)(e), the second authority must provide a written explanation of the difference to—

(a) the carer,

(b) the adult needing care, if the carer asks the authority to do so, and

(c) any other person to whom the carer asks the authority to provide an explanation.

(14) Regulations may specify steps which a local authority must take for the purpose of being satisfied as mentioned in subsection (1)(c), (2)(c) or (3)(c).

(15) In this section—
- (a) an adult's needs are "eligible needs" if they meet the eligibility criteria and are not being met by a carer,
- (b) a reference to moving to an area is a reference to moving to that area with a view to becoming ordinarily resident there, and
- (c) a reference to remaining in an area is a reference to remaining ordinarily resident there.

38 Case where assessments not complete on day of move

(1) If, on the day of the intended move as mentioned in section 37(1)(b), (2)(b) or (3)(b), the second authority has yet to carry out the assessment or assessments under section 37(6), or has done so but has yet to take the other steps required under this Part in the adult's case, it must—
- (a) meet the adult's needs for care and support, and the needs for support of any carer who is continuing as the adult's carer, which the first authority has been meeting, and
- (b) where the first authority has been keeping a care account in the adult's case, itself keep that account on the same basis as the first authority has been keeping it.

(2) The second authority is subject to the duty under subsection (1) until it has—
- (a) carried out the assessment or assessments under section 37(6), and
- (b) taken the other steps required under this Part in the adult's case.

(3) In deciding how to meet the adult's needs for care and support under subsection (1), the second authority must involve—
- (a) the adult,
- (b) any carer who is continuing as the adult's carer, and
- (c) any person whom the adult asks the authority to involve or, where the adult lacks capacity to ask the authority to do that, any person who appears to the authority to be interested in the adult's welfare.

(4) In deciding how to meet the needs for support of any carer who is continuing as the adult's carer, the second authority must involve—
- (a) the carer,
- (b) the adult needing care, if the carer asks the authority to do so, and
- (c) any other person whom the carer asks the authority to involve.

(5) In performing the duty under subsection (3)(a) or (4)(a), the second authority must take all reasonable steps to reach agreement with the adult or carer about how it should meet the needs in question.

(6) The first authority is not required to meet the adult's needs for care and support or, if the adult has a carer, such needs for support as the carer has, for so long as the second authority is subject to the duty under subsection (1).

(7) Where, having complied with the duty under subsection (1), the second authority is not required to meet the adult's needs for care and support under section 18 because the adult is still ordinarily resident in the area of the first authority, the second authority may recover from the first authority the costs it incurs in complying with the duty under subsection (1).

(8) Regulations may specify matters to which the second authority must have regard in deciding how to perform the duty under subsection (1).

Establishing where a person lives, etc.

39 Where a person's ordinary residence is

(1) Where an adult has needs for care and support which can be met only if the adult is living in accommodation of a type specified in regulations, and the adult is living in accommodation in England of a type so specified, the adult is to be treated for the purposes of this Part as ordinarily resident—

(a) in the area in which the adult was ordinarily resident immediately before the adult began to live in accommodation of a type specified in the regulations, or

(b) if the adult was of no settled residence immediately before the adult began to live in accommodation of a type so specified, in the area in which the adult was present at that time.

(2) Where, before beginning to live in his or her current accommodation, the adult was living in accommodation of a type so specified (whether or not of the same type as the current accommodation), the reference in subsection (1)(a) to when the adult began to live in accommodation of a type so specified is a reference to the beginning of the period during which the adult has been living in accommodation of one or more of the specified types for consecutive periods.

(3) The regulations may make provision for determining for the purposes of subsection (1) whether an adult has needs for care and support which can be met only if the adult is living in accommodation of a type specified in the regulations.

(4) An adult who is being provided with accommodation under section 117 of the Mental Health Act 1983 (after-care) is to be treated for the purposes of this Part as ordinarily resident in the area of the local authority in England or the local authority in Wales on which the duty to provide the adult with services under that section is imposed; and for that purpose—

(a) "local authority in England" means a local authority for the purposes of this Part, and

(b) "local authority in Wales" means a local authority for the purposes of the Social Services and Well-being (Wales) Act 2014.

(5) An adult who is being provided with NHS accommodation is to be treated for the purposes of this Part as ordinarily resident—

(a) in the area in which the adult was ordinarily resident immediately before the accommodation was provided, or

(b) if the adult was of no settled residence immediately before the accommodation was provided, in the area in which the adult was present at that time.

(6) "NHS accommodation" means accommodation under—

(a) the National Health Service Act 2006,

(b) the National Health Service (Wales) Act 2006,

(c) the National Health Service (Scotland) Act 1978, or

(d) Article 5(1) of the Health and Personal Social Services (Northern Ireland) Order 1972.

(7) The reference in subsection (1) to this Part does not include a reference to section 28 (independent personal budget).

(8) Schedule 1 (which makes provision about cross-border placements to and from Wales, Scotland or Northern Ireland) has effect.

40 Disputes about ordinary residence or continuity of care

(1) Any dispute about where an adult is ordinarily resident for the purposes of this Part, or any dispute between local authorities under section 37 about the application of that section, is to be determined by—
   (a) the Secretary of State, or
   (b) where the Secretary of State appoints a person for that purpose (the "appointed person"), that person.

(2) The Secretary of State or appointed person may review a determination under subsection (1), provided that the review begins within 3 months of the date of the determination.

(3) Having carried out a review under subsection (2), the Secretary of State or appointed person must—
   (a) confirm the original determination, or
   (b) substitute a different determination.

(4) Regulations may make further provision about resolution of disputes of the type mentioned in subsection (1); the regulations may, for example, include—
   (a) provision for ensuring that care and support is provided to the adult while the dispute is unresolved;
   (b) provision requiring the local authorities in dispute to take specified steps before referring the dispute to the Secretary of State or (as the case may be) the appointed person;
   (c) provision about the procedure for referring the dispute to the Secretary of State or appointed person;
   (d) where a review of a determination has been carried out under subsection (2) and a different determination substituted, provision requiring a local authority to take specified steps (including paying specified amounts) in relation to the period before the determination was substituted.

41 Financial adjustments between local authorities

(1) This section applies where—
   (a) a local authority has been meeting an adult's needs for care and support, but
   (b) it transpires (whether following the determination of a dispute under section 40 or otherwise) that the adult was, for some or all of the time that the authority has been meeting the adult's needs, ordinarily resident in the area of another local authority.

(2) This section also applies where—
   (a) a local authority has been meeting a carer's needs for support, but
   (b) it transpires (whether following the determination of a dispute under section 40 or otherwise) that the adult needing care was, for some or all of the

time that the authority has been meeting the carer's needs, ordinarily resident in the area of another local authority.

(3) The local authority concerned may recover from the other local authority the amount of any payments it made towards meeting the needs in question at a time when the other local authority was instead liable to meet them under section 18 or 20(1) (as the case may be).

(4) Subsection (3) does not apply to payments which are the subject of a deferred payment agreement entered into by the local authority in question, unless it agrees with the other local authority to assign its rights and obligations under the deferred payment agreement to that other authority.

(5) Any period during which a local authority was meeting the needs in question under section 19 or 20(6) is to be disregarded for the purposes of this section.

Safeguarding adults at risk of abuse or neglect

42 Enquiry by local authority

(1) This section applies where a local authority has reasonable cause to suspect that an adult in its area (whether or not ordinarily resident there)—

(a) has needs for care and support (whether or not the authority is meeting any of those needs),

(b) is experiencing, or is at risk of, abuse or neglect, and

(c) as a result of those needs is unable to protect himself or herself against the abuse or neglect or the risk of it.

(2) The local authority must make (or cause to be made) whatever enquiries it thinks necessary to enable it to decide whether any action should be taken in the adult's case (whether under this Part or otherwise) and, if so, what and by whom.

(3) "Abuse" includes financial abuse; and for that purpose "financial abuse" includes—

(a) having money or other property stolen,

(b) being defrauded,

(c) being put under pressure in relation to money or other property, and

(d) having money or other property misused.

43 Safeguarding Adults Boards

(1) Each local authority must establish a Safeguarding Adults Board (an "SAB") for its area.

(2) The objective of an SAB is to help and protect adults in its area in cases of the kind described in section 42(1).

(3) The way in which an SAB must seek to achieve its objective is by co-ordinating and ensuring the effectiveness of what each of its members does.

(4) An SAB may do anything which appears to it to be necessary or desirable for the purpose of achieving its objective.

(5) Schedule 2 (which includes provision about the membership, funding and other resources, strategy and annual report of an SAB) has effect.

(6) Where two or more local authorities exercise their respective duties under subsection (1) by establishing an SAB for their combined area—

(a) a reference in this section, section 44 or Schedule 2 to the authority establishing the SAB is to be read as a reference to the authorities establishing it, and

(b) a reference in this section, that section or that Schedule to the SAB's area is to be read as a reference to the combined area.

44 Safeguarding adults reviews

(1) An SAB must arrange for there to be a review of a case involving an adult in its area with needs for care and support (whether or not the local authority has been meeting any of those needs) if—

(a) there is reasonable cause for concern about how the SAB, members of it or other persons with relevant functions worked together to safeguard the adult, and

(b) condition 1 or 2 is met.

(2) Condition 1 is met if—

(a) the adult has died, and

(b) the SAB knows or suspects that the death resulted from abuse or neglect (whether or not it knew about or suspected the abuse or neglect before the adult died).

(3) Condition 2 is met if—

(a) the adult is still alive, and

(b) the SAB knows or suspects that the adult has experienced serious abuse or neglect.

(4) An SAB may arrange for there to be a review of any other case involving an adult in its area with needs for care and support (whether or not the local authority has been meeting any of those needs).

(5) Each member of the SAB must co-operate in and contribute to the carrying out of a review under this section with a view to—

(a) identifying the lessons to be learnt from the adult's case, and

(b) applying those lessons to future cases.

45 Supply of information

(1) If an SAB requests a person to supply information to it, or to some other person specified in the request, the person to whom the request is made must comply with the request if—

(a) conditions 1 and 2 are met, and

(b) condition 3 or 4 is met.

(2) Condition 1 is that the request is made for the purpose of enabling or assisting the SAB to exercise its functions.

(3) Condition 2 is that the request is made to a person whose functions or activities the SAB considers to be such that the person is likely to have information relevant to the exercise of a function by the SAB.

(4) Condition 3 is that the information relates to—
  (a) the person to whom the request is made,
  (b) a function or activity of that person, or
  (c) a person in respect of whom that person exercises a function or engages in an activity.

(5) Condition 4 is that the information—
  (a) is information requested by the SAB from a person to whom information was supplied in compliance with another request under this section, and
  (b) is the same as, or is derived from, information so supplied.

(6) Information may be used by the SAB, or other person to whom it is supplied under subsection (1), only for the purpose of enabling or assisting the SAB to exercise its functions.

46 Abolition of local authority's power to remove persons in need of care

Section 47 of the National Assistance Act 1948 (which gives a local authority power to remove a person in need of care from home) ceases to apply to persons in England.

47 Protecting property of adults being cared for away from home

(1) This section applies where—
  (a) an adult is having needs for care and support met under section 18 or 19 in a way that involves the provision of accommodation, or is admitted to hospital (or both), and
  (b) it appears to a local authority that there is a danger of loss or damage to movable property of the adult's in the authority's area because—
    (i) the adult is unable (whether permanently or temporarily) to protect or deal with the property, and
    (ii) no suitable arrangements have been or are being made.

(2) The local authority must take reasonable steps to prevent or mitigate the loss or damage.

(3) For the purpose of performing that duty, the local authority—
  (a) may at all reasonable times and on reasonable notice enter any premises which the adult was living in immediately before being provided with accommodation or admitted to hospital, and
  (b) may deal with any of the adult's movable property in any way which is reasonably necessary for preventing or mitigating loss or damage.

(4) A local authority may not exercise the power under subsection (3)(a) unless—
  (a) it has obtained the consent of the adult concerned or, where the adult lacks capacity to give consent, the consent of a person authorised under the Mental Capacity Act 2005 to give it on the adult's behalf, or
  (b) where the adult lacks capacity to give consent and there is no person so authorised, the local authority is satisfied that exercising the power would be in the adult's best interests.

(5) Where a local authority is proposing to exercise the power under subsection (3)(a), the officer it authorises to do so must, if required, produce valid documentation setting out the authorisation to do so.

(6) A person who, without reasonable excuse, obstructs the exercise of the power under subsection (3)(a)—

(a) commits an offence, and

(b) is liable on summary conviction to a fine not exceeding level 4 on the standard scale.

(7) A local authority may recover from an adult whatever reasonable expenses the authority incurs under this section in the adult's case.

Provider failure

48 Temporary duty on local authority

(1) This section applies where a person registered under Chapter 2 of Part 1 of the Health and Social Care Act 2008 (a "registered care provider") in respect of the carrying on of a regulated activity (within the meaning of that Part) becomes unable to carry on that activity because of business failure.

(2) A local authority must for so long as it considers necessary (and in so far as it is not already required to do so) meet those of an adult's needs for care and support and those of a carer's needs for support which were, immediately before the registered care provider became unable to carry on the regulated activity, being met by the carrying on of that activity in the authority's area by the provider.

(3) A local authority is accordingly required to meet needs under subsection (2) regardless of—

(a) whether the relevant adult is ordinarily resident in its area;

(b) whether the authority has carried out a needs assessment, a carer's assessment or a financial assessment;

(c) whether any of the needs meet the eligibility criteria.

(4) Where a local authority is meeting needs under subsection (2), it is not required to carry out a needs assessment, a carer's assessment or a financial assessment or to determine whether any of the needs meet the eligibility criteria.

(5) A local authority may make a charge for meeting needs under subsection (2) (except in so far as doing so involves the provision of information or advice); and a charge under this subsection may cover only the cost that the local authority incurs in meeting the needs to which the charge applies.

(6) Subsection (5) does not apply if section 49 (cross-border cases) applies (see subsection (3) of that section).

(7) If the relevant adult is not ordinarily resident in the area of the local authority which is required to meet needs under subsection (2), that authority—

(a) must, in meeting needs under that subsection which were being met under arrangements made by another local authority, co-operate with that authority (in so far as it is not already required to do so by section 6);

(b) must, in meeting needs under that subsection which were being met under arrangements all or part of the cost of which was paid for by another local authority by means of direct payments, co-operate with that authority (in so far as it is not already required to do so by section 6);

(c) may recover from the other local authority mentioned in paragraph (a) or (b) (as the case may be) the cost it incurs in meeting those of the adult's or carer's needs referred to in the paragraph in question.

(8) Any dispute between local authorities about the application of this section is to be determined under section 40 as if it were a dispute of the type mentioned in subsection (1) of that section.

(9) "The relevant adult" means—

(a) in a case involving an adult's needs for care and support, that adult;

(b) in a case involving a carer's needs for support, the adult needing care.

49 Section 48: cross-border cases

(1) This section applies where, in a case within section 48, immediately before the registered care provider became unable to carry on the regulated activity, some or all of the adult's needs for care and support or the carer's needs for support were being met by the carrying on of that activity by the provider under arrangements made—

(a) by a local authority in Wales discharging its duty under section 35 or 40, or exercising its power under section 36 or 45, of the Social Services and Well-being (Wales) Act 2014,

(b) by a local authority in Scotland discharging its duty under section 12 or 13A of the Social Work (Scotland) Act 1968 or section 25 of the Mental Health (Care and Treatment) (Scotland) Act 2003, or

(c) by a Health and Social Care trust under Article 15 of the Health and Personal Social Services (Northern Ireland) Order 1972 or section 2 of the Carers and Direct Payments Act (Northern Ireland) 2002.

(2) This section also applies where, in a case within section 48—

(a) immediately before the registered care provider became unable to carry on the regulated activity, some or all of the adult's needs for care and support or the carer's needs for support were being met by the carrying on of that activity by the provider, and

(b) all or part of the cost of the accommodation or other services provided by the provider to meet those needs was paid for by means of direct payments made—

(i) under section 50 or 52 of the Social Services and Well-being (Wales) Act 2014,

(ii) as a result of a choice made by the adult pursuant to section 5 of the Social Care (Self-directed Support) (Scotland) Act 2013, or

(iii) by virtue of section 8 of the Carers and Direct Payments Act (Northern Ireland) 2002.

(3) The local authority which is required to meet needs under section 48(2)—

(a) must, in meeting needs under section 48(2) which were being met by the authority which made the arrangements referred to in subsection (1), co-operate with that authority;

(b) must, in meeting needs under section 48(2) which were being met by the provision of accommodation or other services all or part of the cost of which was paid for by an authority by means of direct payments as referred to in subsection (2), co-operate with that authority;

(c) may recover from the authority referred to in paragraph (a) or (b) (as the case may be) the cost it incurs in meeting those of the adult's or carer's needs referred to in the paragraph in question;

(d) may recover from the adult or carer the cost it incurs in meeting those of the adult's or carer's needs other than those referred to in paragraph (a) or (b) (as the case may be).

(4) Any dispute between a local authority and a local authority in Wales, a local authority in Scotland or a Health and Social Care trust about the application of section 48 or of this section is to be resolved in accordance with paragraph 5 of Schedule 1.

(5) "Local authority in Wales" and "local authority in Scotland" each have the meaning given in paragraph 12 of Schedule 1.

(6) The references in paragraphs (a) and (b) of subsection (3) to an authority are references to a local authority in Wales, a local authority in Scotland or a Health and Social Care trust (as the case may be).

50 Temporary duty on local authority in Wales

(1) This section applies where a person registered under Part 2 of the Care Standards Act 2000 in respect of an establishment or agency—

(a) becomes unable to carry on or manage the establishment or agency because of business failure, and

(b) immediately before becoming unable to do so, was providing an adult with accommodation or other services in Wales under arrangements made—

(i) by a local authority meeting an adult's needs for care and support or a carer's needs for support under this Part,

(ii) by a local authority in Scotland discharging its duty under section 12 or 13A of the Social Work (Scotland) Act 1968 or section 25 of the Mental Health (Care and Treatment) (Scotland) Act 2003, or

(iii) by a Health and Social Care trust under Article 15 of the Health and Personal Social Services (Northern Ireland) Order 1972 or section 2 of the Carers and Direct Payments Act (Northern Ireland) 2002.

(2) This section also applies where a person registered under Part 2 of the Care Standards Act 2000 in respect of an establishment or agency—

(a) becomes unable to carry on or manage the establishment or agency because of business failure, and

(b) immediately before becoming unable to do so, was providing an adult with accommodation or other services in Wales all or part of the cost of which was paid for by means of direct payments made—

(i) under this Part of this Act,

(ii) as a result of a choice made by the adult pursuant to section 5 of the Social Care (Self-directed Support) (Scotland) Act 2013, or

(iii) by virtue of section 8 of the Carers and Direct Payments Act (Northern Ireland) 2002.

(3) The local authority in Wales in whose area the accommodation is situated or the services were provided must for so long as it considers necessary meet those of the adult's needs for care and support or the carer's needs for support which were being met by the registered person by the provision of the accommodation or other services.

(4) A local authority in Wales which is required to meet needs under subsection (3)—

(a) must, in meeting needs under that subsection which were being met by the authority which made the arrangements referred to in subsection (1)(b), co-operate with that authority;

(b) must, in meeting needs under subsection (3) which were being met by the provision of accommodation or other services all or part of the cost of which was paid for by an authority by means of direct payments as referred to in subsection (2)(b), co-operate with that authority;

(c) may recover from the authority referred to in paragraph (a) or (b) (as the case may be) the cost it incurs in meeting those of the adult's or carer's needs referred to in the paragraph in question.

(5) Any dispute about the application of this section is to be resolved in accordance with paragraph 5 of Schedule 1.

(6) "Local authority in Wales" and "local authority in Scotland" each have the meaning given in paragraph 12 of Schedule 1.

(7) The references in paragraphs (a) and (b) of subsection (4) to an authority are references to a local authority, a local authority in Scotland or a Health and Social Care trust (as the case may be).

51 Temporary duty on Health and Social Care trust in Northern Ireland

(1) This section applies where a person registered under Part 3 of the Health and Social Services (Quality, Improvement and Regulation) (Northern Ireland) Order 2003 in respect of an establishment or agency—

(a) becomes unable to carry on or manage the establishment or agency because of business failure, and

(b) immediately before becoming unable to do so, was providing an adult with accommodation or other services in Northern Ireland under arrangements made—

(i) by a local authority meeting an adult's needs for care and support or a carer's needs for support under this Part,

(ii) by a local authority in Wales discharging its duty under section 35 or 40, or exercising its power under section 36 or 45, of the Social Services and Well-being (Wales) Act 2014, or

(iii) by a local authority in Scotland discharging its duty under section 12 or 13A of the Social Work (Scotland) Act 1968 or section 25 of the Mental Health (Care and Treatment) (Scotland) Act 2003.

(2) This section also applies where a person registered under Part 3 of the Health and Personal Social Services (Quality, Improvement and Regulation) (Northern Ireland) Order 2003 in respect of an establishment or agency—

(a) becomes unable to carry on or manage the establishment or agency because of business failure, and

(b) immediately before becoming unable to do so, was providing an adult with accommodation or other services in Northern Ireland, all or part of the cost of which was paid for by means of direct payments made—
(i) under this Part of this Act,
(ii) under section 50 or 52 of the Social Services and Well-being (Wales) Act 2014, or
(iii) as a result of a choice made by the adult pursuant to section 5 of the Social Care (Self-directed Support) (Scotland) Act 2013.

(3) The Health and Social Care trust in whose area the accommodation is situated or the services were provided must for so long as it considers necessary meet those of the adult's needs for care and support or the carer's needs for support which were being met by the registered person by the provision of the accommodation or other services.

(4) A Health and Social Care trust which is required to meet needs under subsection (3)—
(a) must, in meeting needs under that subsection which were being met by the authority which made the arrangements referred to in subsection (1)(b), co-operate with that authority;
(b) must, in meeting needs under subsection (3) which were being met by the provision of accommodation or other services all or part of the cost of which was paid for by an authority by means of direct payments as referred to in subsection (2)(b), co-operate with that authority;
(c) may recover from the authority referred to in paragraph (a) or (b) (as the case may be) the cost it incurs in meeting those of the adult's or carer's needs referred to in the paragraph in question.

(5) Any dispute about the application of this section is to be resolved in accordance with paragraph 5 of Schedule 1.

(6) "Local authority in Wales" and "local authority in Scotland" each have the meaning given in paragraph 12 of Schedule 1.

(7) The references in paragraphs (a) and (b) of subsection (4) to an authority are references to a local authority, a local authority in Wales or a local authority in Scotland (as the case may be).

52 Sections 48 to 51: supplementary

(1) An authority becomes subject to the duty under section 48(2), 50(3) or 51(3) as soon as it becomes aware of the business failure.

(2) Section 8 (how to meet needs) applies to meeting needs under section 48(2) as it applies to meeting needs under section 18.

(3) Section 34 of the Social Services and Well-being (Wales) Act 2014 (how to meet needs) applies to meeting needs under section 50(3) as it applies to meeting needs under section 35 of that Act.

(4) In deciding how to meet an adult's needs for care and support under section 48(2), 50(3) or 51(3), an authority must involve—
(a) the adult,
(b) any carer that the adult has, and

(c) any person whom the adult asks the authority to involve or, where the adult lacks capacity to ask the authority to do that, any person who appears to the authority to be interested in the adult's welfare.

(5) In deciding how to meet a carer's needs for support under section 48(2), 50(3) or 51(3), an authority must involve—

(a) the carer, and

(b) any person whom the carer asks the authority to involve.

(6) In carrying out the duty under subsection (4)(a) or (5)(a), an authority must take all reasonable steps to reach agreement with the adult or carer about how it should meet the needs in question.

(7) Sections 21 to 23 (exceptions to duty to meet needs) apply to meeting needs under section 48(2) as they apply to meeting needs under section 18.

(8) Sections 46 to 49 of the Social Services and Well-being (Wales) Act 2014 (exceptions to, and restrictions on, duty to meet needs) apply to meeting needs under section 50(3) as they apply to meeting needs under section 35 of that Act.

(9) Where an adult whose case comes within section 48 is being provided with NHS continuing healthcare under arrangements made by a clinical commissioning group no part of whose area is in the local authority's area, the group is to be treated as a relevant partner of the authority for the purposes of sections 6 and 7.

(10) "NHS continuing healthcare" is to be construed in accordance with standing rules under section 6E of the National Health Service Act 2006.

(11) Where a local authority considers it necessary to do so for the purpose of carrying out its duty under section 48(2), it may request the registered care provider, or such other person involved in the provider's business as it considers appropriate, to provide it with specified information.

(12) Regulations must make provision as to the interpretation for the purposes of sections 48, 50 and 51 and this section of references to business failure or to being unable to do something because of business failure; and the regulations may, in particular, specify circumstances in which a person is to be treated as unable to do something because of business failure.

(13) Pending the commencement of Part 4 of the Social Services and Well-being (Wales) Act 2014—

(a) a reference in section 49 or 51 to making arrangements to meet needs under section 35 or 36 of that Act is to be read as a reference to making arrangements or providing services under—

(i) Part 3 of the National Assistance Act 1948,

(ii) section 45 of the Health Services and Public Health Act 1968,

(iii) section 117 of the Mental Health Act 1983, or

(iv) Schedule 15 to the National Health Service (Wales) Act 2006;

(b) a reference in section 49 or 51 to making arrangements to meet needs under section 40 or 45 of that Act is to be read as a reference to providing services as referred to in section 2 of the Carers and Disabled Children Act 2000;

(c) a reference in section 49 or 51 to making direct payments under section 50 or 52 of that Act is to be read as a reference to making direct payments by virtue of section 57 of the Health and Social Care Act 2001;

(d) subsection (8) is to be read as if there were substituted for it—

"(8) Sections 21(1A) and (8) and 29(6) of the National Assistance Act 1948 apply to meeting needs under section 50(3) as they apply to the exercise of functions under sections 21 and 29 of that Act by a local authority in Wales (within the meaning given in paragraph 12 of Schedule 1)."

(14) Pending the commencement of section 5 of the Social Care (Self-directed Support) (Scotland) Act 2013—

(a) sections 49(2)(b)(ii) and 50(2)(b)(ii) are to be read as if there were substituted for each of them—

"(ii) under section 12B of the Social Work (Scotland) Act 1968,", and

(b) section 51(2)(b)(iii) is to be read as if there were substituted for it—

"(iii) under section 12B of the Social Work (Scotland) Act 1968.".

Market oversight

53 Specifying criteria for application of market oversight regime

(1) Regulations must specify criteria for determining whether (subject to regulations under subsection (4)) section 55 (financial sustainability assessment) applies to a registered care provider who is registered in respect of the carrying on of a regulated activity relating to the provision of social care for adults.

(2) In specifying the criteria, the Secretary of State must have regard to the following in particular—

(a) the amount of social care provided by a registered care provider,

(b) the geographical concentration of a registered care provider's business,

(c) the extent to which a registered care provider specialises in the provision of particular types of care.

(3) The Secretary of State must—

(a) at such times as the Secretary of State considers appropriate, review the criteria for the time being specified in the regulations, and

(b) publish information about how the matters mentioned in subsection (2), and any other matters to which the Secretary of State has regard in specifying the criteria, are to be measured.

(4) Regulations may provide that section 55 does not apply, or applies only to the extent specified, to a specified registered care provider or to a registered care provider of a specified description, regardless of whether that provider or a provider of that description would satisfy the criteria.

(5) Regulations may provide that section 55 applies, or applies to the extent specified, to a specified registered care provider or to a registered care provider of a specified description, regardless of whether that provider or a provider of that description would satisfy the criteria.

(6) The circumstances in which regulations may be made under subsection (4) include those in which the Secretary of State is satisfied that certain registered care providers

are already subject to a regulatory regime comparable to that provided for by sections 55 and 56; and regulations made in such circumstances may, for example, make provision requiring specified persons to co-operate or to share information of a specified description.

(7) "Social care" has the same meaning as in Part 1 of the Health and Social Care Act 2008.

54 Determining whether criteria apply to care provider

(1) The Care Quality Commission must determine, in the case of each registered care provider, whether the provider satisfies one or more of the criteria specified in regulations under section 53.

(2) If the Commission determines that the provider satisfies one or more of the criteria, section 55 applies to that provider unless, or except in so far as, regulations under section 53(4) provide that it does not apply.

(3) Where section 55 applies to a registered care provider (whether as a result of subsection (2) or as a result of regulations under section 53(5)), the Commission must inform the provider accordingly.

55 Assessment of financial sustainability of care provider

(1) Where this section applies to a registered care provider, the Care Quality Commission must assess the financial sustainability of the provider's business of carrying on the regulated activity in respect of which it is registered.

(2) Where the Commission, in light of an assessment under subsection (1), considers that there is a significant risk to the financial sustainability of the provider's business, it may—

(a) require the provider to develop a plan for how to mitigate or eliminate the risk;

(b) arrange for, or require the provider to arrange for, a person with appropriate professional expertise to carry out an independent review of the business.

(3) Where the Commission imposes a requirement on a care provider under subsection (2)(a), it may also require the provider—

(a) to co-operate with it in developing the plan, and

(b) to obtain its approval of the finalised plan.

(4) Where the Commission arranges for a review under subsection (2)(b), it may recover from the provider such costs as the Commission incurs in connection with the arrangements (other than its administrative costs in making the arrangements).

(5) Regulations may make provision for enabling the Commission to obtain from such persons as it considers appropriate information which the Commission believes will assist it to assess the financial sustainability of a registered care provider to which this section applies.

(6) Regulations may make provision about the making of the assessment required by subsection (1).

(7) The Commission may consult such persons as it considers appropriate on the method for assessing the financial sustainability of a registered care provider's business; and,

having done so, it must publish guidance on the method it expects to apply in making the assessment.

56 Informing local authorities where failure of care provider likely

(1) This section applies where the Care Quality Commission is satisfied that a registered care provider to which section 55 applies is likely to become unable to carry on the regulated activity in respect of which it is registered because of business failure as mentioned in section 48.

(2) The Commission must inform the local authorities which it thinks will be required to carry out the duty under section 48(2) if the provider becomes unable to carry on the regulated activity in question.

(3) Where the Commission considers it necessary to do so for the purpose of assisting a local authority to carry out the duty under section 48(2), it may request the provider, or such other person involved in the provider's business as the Commission considers appropriate, to provide it with specified information.

(4) Where (as a result of subsection (3) or otherwise) the Commission has information about the provider's business that it considers may assist a local authority in carrying out the duty under section 48(2), the Commission must give the information to the local authority.

(5) Regulations may make provision as to the circumstances in which the Commission is entitled to be satisfied for the purposes of subsection (1) that a registered care provider is likely to become unable to carry on a regulated activity.

(6) The Commission may consult such persons as it considers appropriate on the methods to apply in assessing likelihood for the purposes of subsection (1); and, having carried out that consultation, it must publish guidance on the methods it expects to apply in making the assessment.

57 Sections 54 to 56: supplementary

(1) For the purposes of Part 1 of the Health and Social Care Act 2008, the duties imposed on the Care Quality Commission under sections 54(1) and 55(1) are to be treated as regulatory functions of the Commission.

(2) For the purposes of that Part of that Act, the doing by the Commission of anything for the purpose of assisting a local authority to carry out the duty under section 48(2) is to be treated as one of the Commission's regulatory functions.

(3) For the purposes of sections 17 and 18 of that Act (cancellation or suspension of registration under Part 1 of that Act), a requirement imposed on a registered care provider under or by virtue of any of sections 54 to 56 (or by virtue of subsection (1) or (2)) is to be treated as a requirement imposed by or under Chapter 6 of Part 1 of that Act.

(4) The Commission must, in exercising any of its functions under sections 54 to 56, have regard to the need to minimise the burdens it imposes on others.

Transition for children to adult care and support, etc.

58 Assessment of a child's needs for care and support

(1) Where it appears to a local authority that a child is likely to have needs for care and support after becoming 18, the authority must, if it is satisfied that it would be of significant benefit to the child to do so and if the consent condition is met, assess—

(a) whether the child has needs for care and support and, if so, what those needs are, and

(b) whether the child is likely to have needs for care and support after becoming 18 and, if so, what those needs are likely to be.

(2) An assessment under subsection (1) is referred to in this Part as a "child's needs assessment".

(3) The consent condition is met if—

(a) the child has capacity or is competent to consent to a child's needs assessment being carried out and the child does so consent, or

(b) the child lacks capacity or is not competent so to consent but the authority is satisfied that carrying out a child's needs assessment would be in the child's best interests.

(4) Where a child refuses a child's needs assessment and the consent condition is accordingly not met, the local authority must nonetheless carry out the assessment if the child is experiencing, or is at risk of, abuse or neglect.

(5) Where a local authority, having received a request to carry out a child's assessment from the child concerned or a parent or carer of the child, decides not to comply with the request, it must give the person who made the request—

(a) written reasons for its decision, and

(b) information and advice about what can be done to prevent or delay the development by the child of needs for care and support in the future.

(6) "Parent", in relation to a child, includes—

(a) a parent of the child who does not have parental responsibility for the child, and

(b) a person who is not a parent of the child but who has parental responsibility for the child.

(7) "Carer", in relation to a child, means a person, other than a parent, who is providing care for the child, whether or not under or by virtue of a contract or as voluntary work.

(8) The reference to providing care includes a reference to providing practical or emotional support.

59 Child's needs assessment: requirements etc.

(1) A child's needs assessment must include an assessment of—

(a) the impact on the matters specified in section 1(2) of what the child's needs for care and support are likely to be after the child becomes 18,

(b) the outcomes that the child wishes to achieve in day-to-day life, and

(c) whether, and if so to what extent, the provision of care and support could contribute to the achievement of those outcomes.

(2) A local authority, in carrying out a child's needs assessment, must involve—

- (a) the child,
- (b) the child's parents and any carer that the child has, and
- (c) any person whom the child or a parent or carer of the child requests the local authority to involve.

(3) When carrying out a child's needs assessment, a local authority must also consider whether, and if so to what extent, matters other than the provision of care and support could contribute to the achievement of the outcomes that the child wishes to achieve in day-to-day life.

(4) Having carried out a child's needs assessment, a local authority must give the child—

- (a) an indication as to whether any of the needs for care and support which it thinks the child is likely to have after becoming 18 are likely to meet the eligibility criteria (and, if so, which ones are likely to do so), and
- (b) advice and information about—
  - (i) what can be done to meet or reduce the needs which it thinks the child is likely to have after becoming 18;
  - (ii) what can be done to prevent or delay the development by the child of needs for care and support in the future.

(5) But in a case where the child is not competent or lacks capacity to understand the things which the local authority is required to give under subsection (4), that subsection is to have effect as if for "must give the child" there were substituted "must give the child's parents".

(6) Where a person to whom a child's needs assessment relates becomes 18, the local authority must decide whether to treat the assessment as a needs assessment; and if the authority decides to do so, this Part applies to the child's needs assessment as if it were a needs assessment that had been carried out after the person had become 18.

(7) In considering what to decide under subsection (6), a local authority must have regard to—

- (a) when the child's needs assessment was carried out, and
- (b) whether it appears to the authority that the circumstances of the person to whom the child's needs assessment relates have changed in a way that might affect the assessment.

(8) "Carer" has the same meaning as in section 58.

60 Assessment of a child's carer's needs for support

(1) Where it appears to a local authority that a carer of a child is likely to have needs for support after the child becomes 18, the authority must, if it is satisfied that it would be of significant benefit to the carer to do so, assess—

- (a) whether the carer has needs for support and, if so, what those needs are, and
- (b) whether the carer is likely to have needs for support after the child becomes 18 and, if so, what those needs are likely to be.

(2) An assessment under subsection (1) is referred to in this Part as a "child's carer's assessment".

(3) Where a child's carer refuses a child's carer's assessment, the local authority is not required to carry out the assessment (and subsection (1) does not apply in the carer's case).

(4) Where, having refused a child's carer's assessment, a child's carer requests the assessment, subsection (1) applies in the carer's case (and subsection (3) does not).

(5) Where a child's carer has refused a child's carer's assessment and the local authority concerned thinks that the carer's needs or circumstances have changed, subsection (1) applies in the carer's case (but subject to further refusal as mentioned in subsection (3)).

(6) Where a local authority, having received a request to carry out a child's carer's assessment from the carer concerned, decides not to comply with the request, it must give the carer—

(a) written reasons for its decision, and

(b) information and advice about what can be done to prevent or delay the development by the carer of needs for support in the future.

(7) "Carer", in relation to a child, means an adult (including one who is a parent of the child) who provides or intends to provide care for the child (but see subsection (8)).

(8) An adult is not a carer for the purposes of this section if the adult provides or intends to provide care—

(a) under or by virtue of a contract, or

(b) as voluntary work.

(9) But in a case where the local authority considers that the relationship between the child and the adult providing or intending to provide care is such that it would be appropriate for the adult to be regarded as a carer, the adult is to be regarded as such (and subsection (8) is therefore to be ignored in that case).

(10) The references to providing care include a reference to providing practical or emotional support.

61 Child's carer's assessment: requirements etc.

(1) A child's carer's assessment must include an assessment of—

(a) whether the carer is able to provide care for the child and is likely to continue to be able to do so after the child becomes 18,

(b) whether the carer is willing to do so and is likely to continue to be willing to do so after the child becomes 18,

(c) the impact on the matters specified in section 1(2) of what the carer's needs for support are likely to be after the child becomes 18,

(d) the outcomes that the carer wishes to achieve in day-to-day life, and

(e) whether, and if so to what extent, the provision of support could contribute to the achievement of those outcomes.

(2) A local authority, in carrying out a child's carer's assessment, must have regard to—

(a) whether the carer works or wishes to do so, and

(b) whether the carer is participating in or wishes to participate in education, training or recreation.

(3) A local authority, in carrying out a child's carer's assessment, must involve—

(a) the carer, and

(b) any person whom the carer asks the local authority to involve.

(4) When carrying out a child's carer's assessment, a local authority must also consider whether, and if so to what extent, matters other than the provision of support could contribute to the achievement of the outcomes that the carer wishes to achieve in day-to-day life.

(5) Having carried out a child's carer's assessment, a local authority must give the carer—

(a) an indication as to whether any of the needs for support which it thinks the carer is likely to have after the child becomes 18 are likely to meet the eligibility criteria (and, if so, which ones are likely to do so), and

(b) advice and information about—

(i) what can be done to meet or reduce the needs which it thinks the carer is likely to have after the child becomes 18;

(ii) what can be done to prevent or delay the development by the carer of needs for support in the future.

(6) Where, in the case of a carer to whom a child's carer's assessment relates, the child becomes 18, the local authority must decide whether to treat the assessment as a carer's assessment; and if the authority decides to do so, this Part applies to the child's carer's assessment as if it were a carer's assessment that had been carried out after the child had become 18.

(7) In considering what to decide under subsection (6), a local authority must have regard to—

(a) when the child's carer's assessment was carried out, and

(b) whether it appears to the authority that the circumstances of the carer to whom the child's carer's assessment relates have changed in a way that might affect the assessment.

(8) "Carer" has the same meaning as in section 60.

62 Power to meet child's carer's needs for support

(1) Where a local authority, having carried out a child's carer's assessment, is satisfied that the carer has needs for support, it may meet such of those needs as it considers appropriate.

(2) Regulations may make provision in connection with the exercise of the power under subsection (1); the regulations may, in particular, provide for provisions of this Part to apply with such modifications as may be specified.

(3) In deciding whether or how to exercise the power under subsection (1), a local authority must have regard to any services being provided to the carer under section 17 of the Children Act 1989.

(4) "Carer" has the same meaning as in section 60.

63 Assessment of a young carer's needs for support

(1) Where it appears to a local authority that a young carer is likely to have needs for support after becoming 18, the authority must, if it is satisfied that it would be of significant benefit to the young carer to do so and if the consent condition is met, assess—

(a) whether the young carer has needs for support and, if so, what those needs are, and

(b) whether the young carer is likely to have needs for support after becoming 18 and, if so, what those needs are likely to be.

(2) An assessment under subsection (1) is referred to in this Part as a "young carer's assessment".

(3) The consent condition is met if—

(a) the young carer has capacity or is competent to consent to a young carer's assessment being carried out and the young carer does so consent, or

(b) the young carer lacks capacity or is not competent so to consent but the authority is satisfied that carrying out a young carer's assessment would be in the young carer's best interests.

(4) Where a young carer refuses a young carer's assessment and the consent condition is accordingly not met, the local authority must nonetheless carry out the assessment if the young carer is experiencing, or is at risk of, abuse or neglect.

(5) Where a local authority, having received a request to carry out a young carer's assessment from the young carer concerned or a parent of the young carer, decides not to comply with the request, it must give the person who made the request—

(a) written reasons for its decision, and

(b) advice and information about what can be done to prevent or delay the development by the young carer of needs for support in the future.

(6) "Young carer" means a person under 18 who provides or intends to provide care for an adult (but see subsection (7)).

(7) A person is not a young carer for the purposes of this section if the person provides or intends to provide care—

(a) under or by virtue of a contract, or

(b) as voluntary work.

(8) But in a case where the local authority considers that the relationship between the adult and the person under 18 providing or intending to provide care is such that it would be appropriate for the person under 18 to be regarded as a young carer, that person is to be regarded as such (and subsection (7) is therefore to be ignored in that case).

(9) The references to providing care include a reference to providing practical or emotional support.

64 Young carer's assessment: requirements etc.

(1) A young carer's assessment must include an assessment of—

(a) whether the young carer is able to provide care for the person in question and is likely to continue to be able to do so after becoming 18,

(b) whether the young carer is willing to do so and is likely to continue to be willing to do so after becoming 18,

(c) the impact on the matters specified in section 1(2) of what the young carer's needs for support are likely to be after the young carer becomes 18,

(d) the outcomes that the young carer wishes to achieve in day-to-day life, and

(e) whether, and if so to what extent, the provision of support could contribute to the achievement of those outcomes.

(2) A local authority, in carrying out a young carer's assessment, must have regard to—

(a) the extent to which the young carer works or wishes to work (or is likely to wish to do so after becoming 18),

(b) the extent to which the young carer is participating in or wishes to participate in education, training or recreation (or is likely to wish to do so after becoming 18).

(3) A local authority, in carrying out a young carer's assessment, must involve—

(a) the young carer,

(b) the young carer's parents, and

(c) any person whom the young carer or a parent of the young carer requests the authority to involve.

(4) When carrying out a young carer's assessment, a local authority must also consider whether, and if so to what extent, matters other than the provision of support could contribute to the achievement of the outcomes that the young carer wishes to achieve in day-to-day life.

(5) Having carried out a young carer's assessment, a local authority must give the young carer—

(a) an indication as to whether any of the needs for support which it thinks the young carer is likely to have after becoming 18 are likely to meet the eligibility criteria (and, if so, which ones are likely to do so), and

(b) advice and information about—

(i) what can be done to meet or reduce the needs for support which it thinks the young carer is likely to have after becoming 18;

(ii) what can be done to prevent or delay the development by the young carer of needs for support in the future.

(6) But in a case where the young carer is not competent or lacks capacity to understand the things which the local authority is required to give under subsection (5), that subsection is to have effect as if for "must give the young carer" there were substituted "must give the young carer's parents".

(7) Where a person to whom a young carer's assessment relates becomes 18, the local authority must decide whether to treat the assessment as a carer's assessment; and if the authority decides to do so, this Part applies to the young carer's assessment as if it were a carer's assessment that had been carried out after the person had become 18.

(8) In considering what to decide under subsection (7), a local authority must have regard to—

(a) when the young carer's assessment was carried out, and

(b) whether it appears to the authority that the circumstances of the person to whom the young carer's assessment relates have changed in a way that might affect the assessment.

65 Assessments under sections 58 to 64: further provision

(1) Regulations under section 12—

(a) may make such provision about carrying out a child's needs assessment as they may make about carrying out a needs assessment;

(b) may make such provision about carrying out a child's carer's assessment or a young carer's assessment as they may make about carrying out a carer's assessment.

(2) A local authority may combine a child's needs assessment or young carer's assessment with an assessment it is carrying out (whether or not under this Part) in relation to another person only if the consent condition is met in relation to the child to whom the child's needs or young carer's assessment relates and—

(a) where the combination would include an assessment relating to another child, the consent condition is met in relation to that other child;

(b) where the combination would include an assessment relating to an adult, the adult agrees.

(3) A local authority may combine a child's carer's assessment with an assessment it is carrying out (whether or not under this Part) in relation to another person only if the adult to whom the child's carer's assessment relates agrees and—

(a) where the combination would include an assessment relating to another adult, that other adult agrees, and

(b) where the combination would include an assessment relating to a child, the consent condition is met in relation to that child.

(4) The consent condition is met in relation to a child if—

(a) the child has capacity or is competent to agree to the assessments being combined and does so agree, or

(b) the child lacks capacity or is not competent so to agree but the local authority is satisfied that combining the assessments would be in the child's best interests.

(5) Where a local authority is carrying out a child's needs assessment, a child's carer's assessment or a young carer's assessment, and there is some other assessment being or about to be carried out in relation to the person to whom the assessment relates or in relation to a relevant person, the local authority may carry out that other assessment—

(a) on behalf of or jointly with the body responsible for carrying it out, or

(b) if that body has arranged to carry out the other assessment jointly with another person, jointly with that body and the other person.

(6) A reference to an assessment includes a reference to part of an assessment.

(7) A person is a "relevant person", in relation to a child's needs, child's carer's or young carer's assessment, if it would be reasonable to combine an assessment relating to that person with the child's needs, child's carer's or young carer's assessment (as mentioned in subsections (2) and (3)).

66 Continuity of services under other legislation

(1) Before section 17A of the Children Act 1989 insert—

"17ZH Section 17 services: transition for children to adult care and support

(1) Subsections (2) to (4) apply where a local authority in England providing services for a child in need in the exercise of functions conferred by section 17—

(a) are required by section 58(1) or 63(1) of the Care Act 2014 to carry out a child's needs assessment or young carer's assessment in relation to the child, or

(b) are required by section 60(1) of that Act to carry out a child's carer's assessment in relation to a carer of the child.

(2) If the local authority carry out the assessment before the child reaches the age of 18 and decide to treat it as a needs or carer's assessment in accordance with section 59(6), 61(6) or 64(7) of the Care Act 2014 (with Part 1 of that Act applying to the assessment as a result), the authority must continue to comply with section 17 after the child reaches the age of 18 until they reach a conclusion in his case.

(3) If the local authority carry out the assessment before the child reaches the age of 18 but decide not to treat it as a needs or carer's assessment in accordance with section 59(6), 61(6) or 64(7) of the Care Act 2014—

(a) they must carry out a needs or carer's assessment (as the case may be) after the child reaches the age of 18, and

(b) they must continue to comply with section 17 after he reaches that age until they reach a conclusion in his case.

(4) If the local authority do not carry out the assessment before the child reaches the age of 18, they must continue to comply with section 17 after he reaches that age until—

(a) they decide that the duty under section 9 or 10 of the Care Act 2014 (needs or carer's assessment) does not apply, or

(b) having decided that the duty applies and having discharged it, they reach a conclusion in his case.

(5) Subsection (6) applies where a local authority in England providing services for a child in need in the exercise of functions conferred by section 17—

(a) receive a request for a child's needs assessment or young carer's assessment to be carried out in relation to the child or for a child's carer's assessment to be carried out in relation to a carer of the child, but

(b) have yet to be required by section 58(1), 60(1) or 63(1) of the Care Act 2014 to carry out the assessment.

(6) If the local authority do not decide, before the child reaches the age of 18, whether or not to comply with the request, they must continue to comply with section 17 after he reaches that age until—

(a) they decide that the duty under section 9 or 10 of the Care Act 2014 does not apply, or

(b) having decided that the duty applies and having discharged it, they reach a conclusion in his case.

(7) A local authority reach a conclusion in a person's case when—

(a) they conclude that he does not have needs for care and support or for support (as the case may be), or

(b) having concluded that he has such needs and that they are going to meet some or all of them, they begin to do so, or

(c) having concluded that he has such needs, they conclude that they are not going to meet any of those needs (whether because those needs do not meet the eligibility criteria or for some other reason).

(8) In this section, "child's needs assessment", "child's carer's assessment", "young carer's assessment", "needs assessment", "carer's assessment" and "eligibility criteria" each have the same meaning as in Part 1 of the Care Act 2014.

17ZI Section 17 services: provision after EHC plan no longer maintained

(1) This section applies where a local authority in England providing services for a person in the exercise, by virtue of section 17ZG, of functions conferred by section 17 are required to carry out a needs assessment in that person's case.

(2) If the EHC plan for the person ceases to be maintained before the local authority reach a conclusion in the person's case, they must continue to comply with section 17 until they do reach a conclusion in his case.

(3) The references to the local authority reaching a conclusion in a person's case are to be read with section 17ZH(7).

(4) In this section, "needs assessment" has the same meaning as in Part 1 of the Care Act 2014."

(2) In section 17ZG of that Act (continued provision of services under section 17 where EHC plan maintained), in subsection (2), after "after the EHC plan has ceased to be maintained" insert ", except in so far as the authority is required to do so under section 17ZH or 17ZI".

(3) After section 2 of the Chronically Sick and Disabled Persons Act 1970 insert—

"2A Welfare services: transition for children to adult care and support

(1) Subsections (2) to (4) apply where a local authority in England making arrangements for a disabled child under section 2 are required by section 58(1) of the Care Act 2014 to carry out a child's needs assessment in relation to the child.

(2) If the local authority carry out the assessment before the child reaches the age of 18 and decide to treat it as a needs assessment in accordance with section 59(6) of the Care Act 2014 (with Part 1 of that Act applying to the assessment as a result), the authority must continue to comply with section 2 after the child reaches the age of 18 until they reach a conclusion in his case.

(3) If the local authority carry out the assessment before the child reaches the age of 18 but decide not to treat it as a needs assessment in accordance with section 59(6) of that Act—

(a) they must carry out a needs assessment after the child reaches the age of 18, and

(b) they must continue to comply with section 2 after he reaches that age until they reach a conclusion in his case.

(4) If the local authority do not carry out the assessment before the child reaches the age of 18, they must continue to comply with section 2 after he reaches that age until—

(a) they decide that the duty under section 9 of the Care Act 2014 (needs assessment) does not apply, or

(b) having decided that the duty applies and having discharged it, they reach a conclusion in his case.

(5) Subsection (6) applies where a local authority in England making arrangements for a disabled child under section 2—

(a) receive a request for a child's needs assessment to be carried out in relation to the child, but

(b) have yet to be required by section 58(1) of the Care Act 2014 to carry out the assessment.

(6) If the local authority do not decide, before the child reaches the age of 18, whether or not to comply with the request, they must continue to comply with section 2 after he reaches that age until—

(a) they decide that the duty under section 9 of the Care Act 2014 does not apply, or

(b) having decided that the duty applies and having discharged it, they reach a conclusion in his case.

(7) A local authority reach a conclusion in a person's case when—

(a) they conclude that he does not have needs for care and support,

(b) having concluded that he has such needs and that they are going to meet some or all of them, they begin to do so, or

(c) having concluded that he has such needs, they conclude that they are not going to meet any of those needs (whether because those needs do not meet the eligibility criteria or for some other reason).

(8) In this section, "child's needs assessment", "needs assessment" and "eligibility criteria" each have the same meaning as in Part 1 of the Care Act 2014."

Independent advocacy support

67 Involvement in assessments, plans etc.

(1) This section applies where a local authority is required by a relevant provision to involve an individual in its exercise of a function.

(2) The authority must, if the condition in subsection (4) is met, arrange for a person who is independent of the authority (an "independent advocate") to be available to represent and support the individual for the purpose of facilitating the individual's involvement; but see subsection (5).

(3) The relevant provisions are—

(a) section 9(5)(a) and (b) (carrying out needs assessment);
(b) section 10(7)(a) (carrying out carer's assessment);
(c) section 25(3)(a) and (b) (preparing care and support plan);
(d) section 25(4)(a) and (b) (preparing support plan);
(e) section 27(2)(b)(i) and (ii) (revising care and support plan);
(f) section 27(3)(b)(i) and (ii) (revising support plan);
(g) section 59(2)(a) and (b) (carrying out child's needs assessment);
(h) section 61(3)(a) (carrying out child's carer's assessment);
(i) section 64(3)(a) and (b) (carrying out young carer's assessment).

(4) The condition is that the local authority considers that, were an independent advocate not to be available, the individual would experience substantial difficulty in doing one or more of the following—
(a) understanding relevant information;
(b) retaining that information;
(c) using or weighing that information as part of the process of being involved;
(d) communicating the individual's views, wishes or feelings (whether by talking, using sign language or any other means).

(5) The duty under subsection (2) does not apply if the local authority is satisfied that there is a person—
(a) who would be an appropriate person to represent and support the individual for the purpose of facilitating the individual's involvement, and
(b) who is not engaged in providing care or treatment for the individual in a professional capacity or for remuneration.

(6) For the purposes of subsection (5), a person is not to be regarded as an appropriate person unless—
(a) where the individual has capacity or is competent to consent to being represented and supported by that person, the individual does so consent, or
(b) where the individual lacks capacity or is not competent so to consent, the local authority is satisfied that being represented and supported by that person would be in the individual's best interests.

(7) Regulations may make provision in connection with the making of arrangements under subsection (2); the regulations may in particular—
(a) specify requirements that must be met for a person to be independent for the purposes of subsection (2);
(b) specify matters to which a local authority must have regard in deciding whether an individual would experience substantial difficulty of the kind mentioned in subsection (4);
(c) specify circumstances in which the exception in subsection (5) does not apply;
(d) make provision as to the manner in which independent advocates are to perform their functions;
(e) specify circumstances in which, if an assessment under this Part is combined with an assessment under this Part that relates to another person, each person may or must be represented and supported by the same independent advocate or by different independent advocates;

(f) provide that an independent advocate may, in such circumstances or subject to such conditions as may be specified, examine and take copies of relevant records relating to the individual.

(8) This section does not restrict the provision that may be made under any other provision of this Act.

(9) "Relevant record" means—

(a) a health record (within the meaning given in section 68 of the Data Protection Act 1998 (as read with section 69 of that Act)),

(b) a record of, or held by, a local authority and compiled in connection with a function under this Part or a social services function (within the meaning given in section 1A of the Local Authority Social Services Act 1970),

(c) a record held by a person registered under Part 2 of the Care Standards Act 2000 or Chapter 2 of Part 1 of the Health and Social Care Act 2008, or

(d) a record of such other description as may be specified in the regulations.

68 Safeguarding enquiries and reviews

(1) This section applies where there is to be—

(a) an enquiry under section 42(2),

(b) a review under section 44(1) of a case in which condition 2 in section 44(3) is met or a review under section 44(4).

(2) The relevant local authority must, if the condition in subsection (3) is met, arrange for a person who is independent of the authority (an "independent advocate") to be available to represent and support the adult to whose case the enquiry or review relates for the purpose of facilitating his or her involvement in the enquiry or review; but see subsections (4) and (6).

(3) The condition is that the local authority considers that, were an independent advocate not to be available, the individual would experience substantial difficulty in doing one or more of the following—

(a) understanding relevant information;

(b) retaining that information;

(c) using or weighing that information as part of the process of being involved;

(d) communicating the individual's views, wishes or feelings (whether by talking, using sign language or any other means).

(4) The duty under subsection (2) does not apply if the local authority is satisfied that there is a person—

(a) who would be an appropriate person to represent and support the adult for the purpose of facilitating the adult's involvement, and

(b) who is not engaged in providing care or treatment for the adult in a professional capacity or for remuneration.

(5) For the purposes of subsection (4), a person is not to be regarded as an appropriate person unless—

(a) where the adult has capacity to consent to being represented and supported by that person, the adult does so consent, or

(b) where the adult lacks capacity so to consent, the local authority is satisfied that being represented and supported by that person would be in the adult's best interests.

(6) If the enquiry or review needs to begin as a matter of urgency, it may do so even if the authority has not yet been able to comply with the duty under subsection (2) (and the authority continues to be subject to the duty).

(7) "Relevant local authority" means—

(a) in a case within subsection (1)(a), the authority making the enquiry or causing it to be made;

(b) in a case within subsection (1)(b), the authority which established the SAB arranging the review.

Enforcement of debts

69 Recovery of charges, interest etc.

(1) Any sum due to a local authority under this Part is recoverable by the authority as a debt due to it.

(2) But subsection (1) does not apply in a case where a deferred payment agreement could, in accordance with regulations under section 34(1), be entered into, unless—

(a) the local authority has sought to enter into such an agreement with the adult from whom the sum is due, and

(b) the adult has refused.

(3) A sum is recoverable under this section—

(a) in a case in which the sum becomes due to the local authority on or after the commencement of this section, within six years of the date the sum becomes due;

(b) in any other case, within three years of the date on which it becomes due.

(4) Where a person misrepresents or fails to disclose (whether fraudulently or otherwise) to a local authority any material fact in connection with the provisions of this Part, the following sums are due to the authority from the person—

(a) any expenditure incurred by the authority as a result of the misrepresentation or failure, and

(b) any sum recoverable under this section which the authority has not recovered as a result of the misrepresentation or failure.

(5) The costs incurred by a local authority in recovering or seeking to recover a sum due to it under this Part are recoverable by the authority as a debt due to it.

(6) Regulations may—

(a) make provision for determining the date on which a sum becomes due to a local authority for the purposes of this section;

(b) specify cases or circumstances in which a sum due to a local authority under this Part is not recoverable by it under this section;

(c) specify cases or circumstances in which a local authority may charge interest on a sum due to it under this Part;

(d) where interest is chargeable, provide that it—

(i) must be charged at a rate specified in or determined in accordance with the regulations, or

(ii) may not be charged at a rate that exceeds the rate specified in or determined in accordance with the regulations.

70 Transfer of assets to avoid charges

(1) This section applies in a case where an adult's needs have been or are being met by a local authority under sections 18 to 20 and where—

(a) the adult has transferred an asset to another person (a "transferee"),

(b) the transfer was undertaken with the intention of avoiding charges for having the adult's needs met, and

(c) either the consideration for the transfer was less than the value of the asset or there was no consideration for the transfer.

(2) The transferee is liable to pay to the local authority an amount equal to the difference between—

(a) the amount the authority would have charged the adult were it not for the transfer of the asset, and

(b) the amount it did in fact charge the adult.

(3) But the transferee is not liable to pay to the authority an amount which exceeds the benefit accruing to the transferee from the transfer.

(4) Where an asset has been transferred to more than one transferee, the liability of each transferee is in proportion to the benefit accruing to that transferee from the transfer.

(5) "Asset" means anything which may be taken into account for the purposes of a financial assessment.

(6) The value of an asset (other than cash) is the amount which would have been realised if it had been sold on the open market by a willing seller at the time of the transfer, with a deduction for—

(a) the amount of any incumbrance on the asset, and

(b) a reasonable amount in respect of the expenses of the sale.

(7) Regulations may specify cases or circumstances in which liability under subsection (2) does not arise.

Review of funding provisions

71 Five-yearly review by Secretary of State

(1) The Secretary of State must review—

(a) the level at which the cap on care costs is for the time being set under regulations under section 15(4),

(b) the level at which the amount attributable to an adult's daily living costs is for the time being set under regulations under section 15(8), and

(c) the level at which the financial limit is for the time being set under regulations under section 17(8).

(2) In carrying out the review, the Secretary of State must have regard to—

(a) the financial burden on the state of each of those matters being at the level in question,
(b) the financial burden on local authorities of each of those matters being at the level in question,
(c) the financial burden on adults who have needs for care and support of each of those matters being at the level in question,
(d) the length of time for which people can reasonably be expected to live in good health,
(e) changes in the ways or circumstances in which adults' needs for care and support are being or are likely to be met,
(f) changes in the prevalence of conditions for which the provision of care and support is or is likely to be required, and
(g) such other factors as the Secretary of State considers relevant.

(3) The Secretary of State must prepare and publish a report on the outcome of the review.

(4) The first report must be published before the end of the period of five years beginning with the day on which section 15 comes into force.

(5) Each subsequent report must be published before the end of the period of five years beginning with the day on which the previous report was published.

(6) The Secretary of State may arrange for some other person to carry out the whole or part of a review under this section on the Secretary of State's behalf.

(7) The Secretary of State must lay before Parliament a report prepared under this section.

Appeals

72 Part 1 appeals

(1) Regulations may make provision for appeals against decisions taken by a local authority in the exercise of functions under this Part in respect of an individual (including decisions taken before the coming into force of the first regulations made under this subsection).

(2) The regulations may in particular make provision about—
(a) who may (and may not) bring an appeal;
(b) grounds on which an appeal may be brought;
(c) pre-conditions for bringing an appeal;
(d) how an appeal is to be brought and dealt with (including time limits);
(e) who is to consider an appeal;
(f) matters to be taken into account (and disregarded) by the person or body considering an appeal;
(g) powers of the person or body deciding an appeal;
(h) what action is to be taken by a local authority as a result of an appeal decision;
(i) providing information about the right to bring an appeal, appeal procedures and other sources of information and advice;
(j) representation and support for an individual bringing or otherwise involved in an appeal;

(k) investigations into things done or not done by a person or body with power to consider an appeal.

(3) Provision about pre-conditions for bringing an appeal may require specified steps to have been taken before an appeal is brought.

(4) Provision about how an appeal is to be dealt with may include provision for—

(a) the appeal to be treated as, or as part of, an appeal brought or complaint made under another procedure;

(b) the appeal to be considered with any such appeal or complaint.

(5) Provision about who is to consider an appeal may include provision—

(a) establishing, or requiring or permitting the establishment of, a panel or other body to consider an appeal;

(b) requiring an appeal to be considered by, or by persons who include, persons with a specified description of expertise or experience.

(6) Provision about representation and support for an individual may include provision applying any provision of or made under section 67, with or without modifications.

(7) The regulations may make provision for—

(a) an appeal brought or complaint made under another procedure to be treated as, or as part of, an appeal brought under the regulations;

(b) an appeal brought or complaint made under another procedure to be considered with an appeal brought under the regulations;

(c) matters raised in an appeal brought under the regulations to be taken into account by the person or body considering an appeal brought or complaint made under another procedure.

(8) The regulations may include provision conferring functions on a person or body established by or under an Act (including an Act passed after the passing of this Act); for that purpose, the regulations may amend, repeal, or revoke an enactment, or provide for an enactment to apply with specified modifications.

(9) Regulations may make provision, in relation to a case where an appeal is brought under regulations under subsection (1)—

(a) for any provision of this Part to apply, for a specified period, as if a decision ("the interim decision") differing from the decision appealed against had been made;

(b) as to what the terms of the interim decision are, or as to how and by whom they are to be determined;

(c) for financial adjustments to be made following a decision on the appeal.

(10) The period specified under subsection (9)(a) may not begin earlier than the date on which the decision appealed against was made, or end later than the date on which the decision on the appeal takes effect.

Miscellaneous

73 Human Rights Act 1998: provision of regulated care or support etc a public function

(1) This section applies where—

(a) in England, a registered care provider provides care and support to an adult or support to a carer, in the course of providing—
   (i) personal care in a place where the adult receiving the personal care is living when the personal care is provided, or
   (ii) residential accommodation together with nursing or personal care;

(b) in Wales, a person registered under Part 2 of the Care Standards Act 2000 provides care and support to an adult, or support to a carer, in the course of providing—
   (i) personal care in a place where the adult receiving the personal care is living when the personal care is provided, or
   (ii) residential accommodation together with nursing or personal care;

(c) in Scotland, a person provides advice, guidance or assistance to an adult or support to a carer, in the course of providing a care service which is registered under section 59 of the Public Services Reform (Scotland) Act 2010 and which consists of the provision of—
   (i) personal care in a place where the adult receiving the personal care is living when the personal care is provided, or
   (ii) residential accommodation together with nursing or personal care;

(d) in Northern Ireland, a person registered under Part 3 of the Health and Personal Social Services (Quality, Improvement and Regulation) (Northern Ireland) Order 2003 provides advice, guidance or assistance to an adult or services to a carer, in the course of providing—
   (i) personal care in a place where the adult receiving the personal care is living when the personal care is provided, or
   (ii) residential accommodation together with nursing or personal care.

In this section "the care or support" means the care and support, support, advice, guidance, assistance or services provided as mentioned above, and "the provider" means the person who provides the care or support.

(2) The provider is to be taken for the purposes of section 6(3)(b) of the Human Rights Act 1998 (acts of public authorities) to be exercising a function of a public nature in providing the care or support, if the requirements of subsection (3) are met.

(3) The requirements are that—

(a) the care or support is arranged by an authority listed in column 1 of the Table below, or paid for (directly or indirectly, and in whole or in part) by such an authority, and

(b) the authority arranges or pays for the care or support under a provision listed in the corresponding entry in column 2 of the Table.

TABLE

Authority	*Provisions imposing duty or conferring power to meet needs*
Local authority in England	Sections 2, 18, 19, 20, 38 and 48 of this Act.
Local authority in Wales	Part 4 and section 189 of the Social Services and Well-being (Wales) Act 2014.

Authority	*Provisions imposing duty or conferring power to meet needs*
	Section 50 of this Act.
Local authority in Scotland	Sections 12, 13A, 13B and 14 of the Social Work (Scotland) Act 1968.
	Section 3 of the Social Care (Self-directed Support) (Scotland) Act 2013.
Health and Social Care trust	Article 15 of the Health and Personal Social Services (Northern Ireland) Order 1972.
	Section 51 of this Act.
Authority (within the meaning of section 10 of the Carers and Direct Payments Act (Northern Ireland) 2002)	Section 2 of the Carers and Direct Payments Act (Northern Ireland) 2002.

(4) In this section—

"local authority in England" means a local authority for the purposes of this Part;

"local authority in Wales" means a local authority for the purposes of the Social Services and Well-being (Wales) Act 2014;

"local authority in Scotland" means a council constituted under section 2 of the Local Government etc. (Scotland) Act 1994;

"nursing care", for England, Wales and Northern Ireland, has the same meaning as in the Health and Social Care Act 2008 (Regulated Activities) Regulations 2010, as amended from time to time;

"personal care"—

(a) for England, Wales and Northern Ireland, has the same meaning as in the Health and Social Care Act 2008 (Regulated Activities) Regulations 2010, as amended from time to time;

(b) for Scotland, has the same meaning as in Part 5 of the Public Services Reform (Scotland) Act 2010, as amended from time to time.

74 Discharge of hospital patients with care and support needs

Schedule 3 (which includes provision about the discharge of hospital patients with care and support needs) has effect.

75 After-care under the Mental Health Act 1983

(1) In section 117 of the Mental Health Act 1983 (after-care), in subsection (2), after "to provide" insert "or arrange for the provision of".

(2) In subsection (2D) of that section, for the words from "as if" to the end substitute "as if the words "provide or" were omitted."

(3) In subsection (3) of that section, after "means the local social services authority" insert "—

Expression	*Provision*
Adult	Section 2(8)
Adult needing care	Section 10(3)
Authority under the Mental Capacity Act 2005	Subsection (3) below
Best interests	Subsection (2) below
Cap on care costs	Section 15(4)
Capacity, having or lacking	Subsection (2) below
Care and support plan	Section 25
Care account	Section 29
Carer (other than in sections 58 to 62)	Section 10(3)
Carer's assessment	Sections 10(2) and 12(8) and (9)
Child's carer's assessment	Section 60(2)
Child's needs assessment	Section 58(2)
Daily living costs, amount attributable to	Section 15(8)
Deferred payment agreement	Section 34
Direct payment	Sections 31 and 32
Eligibility criteria	Section 13
Financial assessment	Section 17(5)
Financial limit	Section 17(10)
Financial year	Section 126
The health service	Section 126
Independent personal budget	Section 28
Local authority	Section 1(4)
Needs assessment	Sections 9(2) and 12(8) and (9)
Parent	Section 58(6)
Personal budget	Section 26
Registered care provider	Section 48
Support plan	Section 25
Well-being	Section 1(2)
Young carer	Section 63(6)
Young carer's assessment	Section 63(2)

(2) A reference in this Part to having or lacking capacity, or to a person's best interests, is to be interpreted in accordance with the Mental Capacity Act 2005.

(3) A reference in this Part to being authorised under the Mental Capacity Act 2005 is a reference to being authorised (whether in general or specific terms) as—

(a) a donee of a lasting power of attorney granted under that Act, or

(b) a deputy appointed by the Court of Protection under section 16(2)(b) of that Act.

PART 2

CARE STANDARDS

Quality of services

81 Duty of candour

In section 20 of the Health and Social Care Act 2008 (regulation of regulated activities), after subsection (5) insert—

"(5A) Regulations under this section must make provision as to the provision of information in a case where an incident of a specified description affecting a person's safety occurs in the course of the person being provided with a service."

82 Warning notice

(1) In section 29 of the Health and Social Care Act 2008 (warning notice), after subsection (1) insert—

"(1A) But a warning notice under this section may not be given to an NHS trust established under section 25 of the National Health Service Act 2006 or an NHS foundation trust."

(2) In subsections (2) and (3)(a) of that section, after "warning notice" insert "under this section".

(3) After that section insert—

"29A Warning notice: quality of health care

(1) If it appears to the Commission that the quality of health care provided by an NHS trust established under section 25 of the National Health Service Act 2006 or by an NHS foundation trust requires significant improvement, the Commission may give the trust a warning notice.

(2) A warning notice under this section is a notice in writing—

(a) stating that the Commission has formed the view that the quality of health care provided by the trust requires significant improvement,

(b) specifying the health care concerned,

(c) giving the Commission's reasons for its view, and

(d) requiring the trust to make a significant improvement to the quality of the health care concerned within a specified time.

(3) Where a warning notice under this section imposes more than one requirement under subsection (2)(d), it may specify different times for different requirements.

(4) The Commission must—

(a) where the notice specifies only one time under subsection (2)(d), determine at the end of that time whether the requirement has been complied with;

(b) where the notice specifies more than one time under subsection (2)(d), determine at the end of the latest of those times, whether the requirements have been complied with.

(5) Where, having carried out the duty under subsection (4), the Commission is satisfied that a requirement to which the notice relates has not been complied with, it—

(a) must decide what action to take in relation to the trust, and

(b) in so deciding in the case of an NHS foundation trust, must consider in particular whether to require Monitor to make an order under section 65D(2) of the National Health Service Act 2006 (appointment of trust special administrator)."

(4) In each of the following provisions of that Act, after "section 29" insert "or 29A"—

(a) section 32(1)(a) (decisions against which appeal may not be made to the First-tier tribunal),

(b) section 39(2)(c) (bodies required to be given certain notices), and

(c) section 89(1)(e) and (2) (publication of information relating to enforcement action).

(5) In section 88(1)(d) of that Act (guidance issued by the Commission about enforcement action), for "section 29" substitute "sections 29 and 29A".

83 Imposition of licence conditions on NHS foundation trusts

(1) Section 111 of the Health and Social Care Act 2012 (imposition by Monitor of licence conditions on NHS foundation trusts during transitional period) is amended as follows.

(2) After subsection (2) insert—

"(2A) Where a warning notice under section 29A of the Health and Social Care Act 2008 is given to an NHS foundation trust, Monitor may include in the trust's licence such conditions as it considers appropriate in connection with the matters to which the notice relates."

(3) In subsections (3) to (5) and (7) to (9), after "subsection (1)" in each place it appears insert "or (2A)".

84 Trust special administration: appointment of administrator

(1) In section 65D of the National Health Service Act 2006 (NHS foundation trusts: appointment of trust special administrator), in subsection (1)—

(a) after "satisfied that" insert "—

(a)",

and

(b) at the end insert ", or

(b) there is a serious failure by an NHS foundation trust to provide services that are of sufficient quality to be provided under this Act and it is appropriate to make an order under subsection (2)."

(2) After that subsection insert—

"(1A) This section also applies if the Care Quality Commission—

(a) is satisfied that there is a serious failure by an NHS foundation trust to provide services that are of sufficient quality to be provided under this Act and that it is appropriate to make an order under subsection (2),

(b) informs the regulator that it is satisfied as mentioned in paragraph (a) and gives the regulator its reasons for being so satisfied, and

(c) requires the regulator to make an order under subsection (2)."

(3) In subsection (2) of that section, after "The regulator may" insert "or, where this section applies as a result of subsection (1A), must".

(4) After subsection (3) of that section insert—

"(3A) Before imposing a requirement as mentioned in subsection (1A)(c), the Care Quality Commission must—

(a) consult the Secretary of State and the regulator, and

(b) having done that, consult—

(i) the trust,

(ii) the Board, and

(iii) any other person to which the trust provides services under this Act and which the Commission considers it appropriate to consult."

(5) In subsection (4) of that section, after "making an order under this section" insert "(except where it is required to do so as a result of subsection (1A))".

(6) In section 65N of that Act (guidance for trust special administrators), after subsection (3) insert—

"(3A) Before publishing guidance under this section, the Secretary of State must consult the Care Quality Commission."

(7) In subsection (4) of that section, for "the reference in subsection (1) to the Secretary of State is to be read as a reference" substitute "the references in subsections (1) and (3A) to the Secretary of State are to be read as references".

(8) In paragraph 24 of Schedule 14 to the Health and Social Care Act 2012 (abolition of NHS trusts in England: consequential amendments to section 65N of the National Health Service Act 2006), after sub-paragraph (2) insert—

"(2A) In subsection (3A), for "the Secretary of State" substitute "the regulator"."

85 Trust special administration: objective, consultation and reports

(1) In section 65DA of the National Health Service Act 2006 (objective of trust special administration), in subsection (1), after paragraph (a) (but before the following "and") insert—

"(aa) that the services whose continuous provision is secured as mentioned in paragraph (a) are of sufficient safety and quality to be provided under this Act,".

(2) After subsection (5) of that section insert—

"(5A) Before publishing guidance under subsection (4)(c), the regulator must consult the Care Quality Commission."

(3) In section 65F of that Act (administrator's draft report), in subsection (2)—

(a) omit the "and" preceding paragraph (b), and

(b) after that paragraph insert ", and

(c) the Care Quality Commission."

(4) In subsection (5) of that section, in paragraph (a), for "65DA" substitute "65DA(1)(a)".

(5) After that subsection insert—

"(5A) Nor, in the case of an NHS foundation trust, may the administrator provide the draft report to the regulator under subsection (1) without having obtained from the Care Quality Commission a statement that it considers that the recommendation in the draft report would achieve that part of the objective set out in section 65DA(1)(aa)."

(6) In subsection (6) of that section—

(a) after "Where the Board" insert "or the Care Quality Commission",

(b) for "to that effect" substitute "to the effect mentioned in subsection (5) or (5A)", and

(c) after ", the Board" insert "or (as the case may be) the Commission".

(7) In section 65G of that Act (consultation plan), in subsection (4), in paragraph (a), for "65DA" substitute "65DA(1)(a)".

(8) After that subsection insert—

"(4A) Nor may the administrator make a variation to the draft report following the consultation period without having obtained from the Care Quality Commission a statement that it considers that the recommendation in the draft report as so varied would achieve that part of the objective set out in section 65DA(1)(aa)."

(9) In subsection (5) of that section—

(a) after "Where the Board" insert "or the Care Quality Commission",

(b) for "to that effect" substitute "to the effect mentioned in subsection (4) or (4A)", and

(c) after ", the Board" insert "or (as the case may be) the Commission".

(10) In section 65H of that Act (consultation requirements)—

(a) in subsection (7), after paragraph (b) insert—

"(ba) the Care Quality Commission;", and

(b) in subsection (9), after "subsection (7)(b)," insert "(ba),".

(11) In section 65KB of that Act (Secretary of State's response to regulator's decision), in subsection (1), after paragraph (c) insert—

"(ca) that the Care Quality Commission has discharged its functions for the purposes of this Chapter,".

(12) In subsection (2) of that section, in paragraph (b), after "the regulator" insert "and the Care Quality Commission".

(13) In section 65KD of that Act (Secretary of State's response to re-submitted final report), in subsection (3), for "(8)" substitute "(8A)".

(14) After subsection (8) of that section insert—

"(8A) If the notice states that the Care Quality Commission has failed to discharge a function—

(a) the Care Quality Commission is to be treated for the purposes of this Act as having failed to discharge the function, and

(b) the failure is to be treated for those purposes as significant (and section 82 of the Health and Social Care Act 2008 applies accordingly)."

(15) In paragraph 15(4) of Schedule 14 to the Health and Social Care Act 2012 (abolition of NHS trusts in England: consequential amendments to section 65F of the National Health Service Act 2006)—

(a) in the new subsection (2A) to be inserted by paragraph 15(4), in paragraph (a), for "65DA" substitute "65DA(1)(a)",

(b) after that new subsection, insert—

"(2AA) Nor may the administrator provide the draft report to the regulator under subsection (1) without having obtained from the Care Quality Commission a statement that it considers that the recommendation in the draft report would achieve that part of the objective set out in section 65DA(1)(aa).", and

(c) in the new subsection (2B) to be inserted by paragraph 15(4)—

(i) after "Where the Board" insert "or the Care Quality Commission",

(ii) for "to that effect" substitute "to the effect mentioned in subsection (2A) or (2AA)", and

(iii) after ", the Board" insert "or (as the case may be) the Commission".

Care Quality Commission

86 Restriction on applications for variation or removal of conditions

(1) Section 19 of the Health and Social Care Act 2008 (applications by registered persons to the Care Quality Commission for variation or removal of conditions, etc.) is amended as follows.

(2) In subsection (1), after "Except in case A or B" insert "and subject to subsections (3A) to (3F)".

(3) After subsection (3) insert—

"(3A) R may not apply under subsection (1)(a) for the variation of a condition where either subsection (3B) or (3C) applies.

(3B) This subsection applies where—

(a) the Commission has given R notice under section 26(4)(c) of a proposal to make that variation (or a variation which would have substantially the same effect as that variation), and

(b) the Commission has not decided not to take that step.

(3C) This subsection applies where—

(a) the Commission has given R notice under section 28(3) of its decision to make that variation (or a variation which would have substantially the same effect as that variation), and

(b) either the time within which an appeal may be brought has not expired or, if an appeal has been brought, it has not yet been determined.

(3D) R may not apply under subsection (1)(a) for the removal of a condition where either subsection (3E) or (3F) applies.

(3E) This subsection applies where—

(a) the Commission has given R notice under section 26(4)(c) of a proposal to remove that condition, and

(b) the Commission has not decided not to take that step.

(3F) This subsection applies where—

(a) the Commission has given R notice under section 28(3) of its decision to remove that condition, and

(b) either the time within which an appeal may be brought has not expired or, if an appeal has been brought, it has not yet been determined."

(4) The amendments made by this section do not affect any application made under section 19(1)(a) of the Health and Social Care Act 2008 before the day on which those amendments come into force.

87 Rights of appeal

(1) In section 26 of the Health and Social Care Act 2008 (registration procedure: notice of proposals), after subsection (4) insert—

"(4A) Where a proposal under subsection (4) names an individual and specifies action that the Commission would require the registered person to take in relation to that individual, the Commission must give that individual notice in writing of the proposal."

(2) In section 28 of that Act (notice of decisions), in subsection (6), for "subsection (7)" substitute "subsections (7) to (9)".

(3) In that section, after subsection (7) insert—

"(8) But in a case where notice of the proposal has been given to an individual under section 26(4A) subsection (7) does not apply unless, by the time the Commission receives the applicant's notification, it has received notification from the individual that he or she does not intend to appeal.

(9) And if the Commission receives notification from the individual after it receives the applicant's notification and before the end of the period mentioned in subsection (6)(a), the decision is to take effect when the Commission receives the individual's notification."

88 Unitary board

(1) In paragraph 3 of Schedule 1 to the Health and Social Care Act 2008 (membership of the Care Quality Commission), in sub-paragraph (1)—

(a) after paragraph (a), omit "and", and

(b) at the end of paragraph (b) insert ",

(c) a chief executive appointed by the members appointed under paragraphs (a) and (b), and

(d) other members appointed by the members appointed under paragraphs (a) and (b)."

(2) After that sub-paragraph, insert—

"(1A) The members appointed under sub-paragraph (1)(a) and (b)—

(a) are not employees of the Commission, and

(b) are referred to in this Schedule as the "non-executive members".

(1B) The members appointed under sub-paragraph (1)(c) and (d)—

(a) are employees of the Commission, and

(b) are referred to in this Schedule as the "executive members".

(1C) The number of non-executive members must exceed the number of executive members."

(3) In sub-paragraph (2) of that paragraph—

(a) for "sub-paragraph (1)", substitute "sub-paragraph (1)(a) and (b)", and

(b) for "the members", substitute "the non-executive members".

(4) In sub-paragraph (3) of that paragraph, for "any other member", substitute "any other non-executive member".

(5) In sub-paragraph (4) of that paragraph—

(a) in paragraph (a)—

(i) for "other members", substitute "other non-executive members", and

(ii) for "of members who may be appointed", substitute "of such members who may be appointed",

(b) after paragraph (a), omit "and",

(c) in paragraph (b), for "other members", substitute "other non-executive members", and

(d) after paragraph (b), insert—

"(c) the limits on the total number of members who may be appointed, and

(d) the minimum total number of members who must be appointed."

(6) In paragraph 4 of that Schedule (the cross-heading preceding which becomes "Remuneration and allowances for non-executive members"), in sub-paragraphs (1) and (2), for "any other member", substitute "any other non-executive member".

(7) In paragraph 5 of that Schedule (employees), omit sub-paragraph (1).

(8) In sub-paragraph (2) of that paragraph, for "such other employees", substitute "such employees (in addition to the executive members appointed by the non-executive members)".

Increasing the independence of the Care Quality Commission

89 Chief Inspectors

After paragraph 3 of Schedule 1 to the Health and Social Care Act 2008 insert—

"*3A Chief Inspectors*

3A (1) The non-executive members must—

(a) appoint an executive member to be the Chief Inspector of Hospitals,

(b) appoint an executive member to be the Chief Inspector of Adult Social Care, and

(c) appoint an executive member to be the Chief Inspector of General Practice.

(2) Each of those executive members is to exercise such functions of the Commission on its behalf as it determines.

(3) When exercising functions under sub-paragraph (2), an executive member must have regard to the importance of safeguarding and promoting the Commission's independence from the Secretary of State."

90 Independence of the Care Quality Commission

(1) Part 1 of the Health and Social Care Act 2008 (the Care Quality Commission) is amended as follows.

(2) In section 48 (special reviews or investigations), omit subsection (7) (Secretary of State's power to make regulations as to procedure for representations before publication of report).

(3) In section 54 (studies as to economy, efficiency etc), in subsections (1) and (3), omit ", with the approval of the Secretary of State,".

(4) After subsection (2) of that section, insert—

"(2A) The Commission may not exercise the power under subsection (1)(a), so far as it relates to the activity mentioned in subsection (2)(d), without the approval of the Secretary of State."

(5) In section 55 (publication of results of studies under section 54), omit subsection (2) (Secretary of State's power to make regulations as to procedure for representations before publication of report).

(6) In section 57 (reviews of data, studies and research), in subsection (1), omit ", with the approval of the Secretary of State,".

(7) In section 61 (inspections carried out for registration purposes), omit—

(a) subsection (1) (Secretary of State's power to make regulations specifying frequency etc. of inspections), and

(b) subsection (4) (Secretary of State's power to make regulations as to procedure for representations before publication of report).

(8) In section 83 (annual reports), omit subsection (3) (Secretary of State's power to direct preparation of separate reports).

(9) In paragraph 5 of Schedule 4 (inspection programmes etc.), omit—

(a) in sub-paragraph (1) (preparation of programme etc.), ", or at such times as the Secretary of State may specify by order,", and

(b) sub-paragraph (3) (Secretary of State's power to specify form of programme etc.).

(10) In consequence of subsections (3) and (6), omit section 293(3) and (4) of the Health and Social Care Act 2012.

Performance ratings

91 Reviews and performance assessments

(1) Chapter 3 of Part 1 of the Health and Social Care Act 2008 (the Care Quality Commission: quality of health and social care) is amended as follows.

(2) For section 46 (periodic reviews of health and social care provision) substitute—

"46 Reviews and performance assessments

(1) The Commission must, in respect of such regulated activities and such registered service providers as may be prescribed—

(a) conduct reviews of the carrying on of the regulated activities by the service providers,

(b) assess the performance of the service providers following each such review, and

(c) publish a report of its assessment.

(2) Regulations under subsection (1) may prescribe—

(a) all regulated activities or regulated activities of a particular description;

(b) all registered service providers or particular registered service providers;

(c) the whole of a regulated activity or a particular aspect of it.

(3) The assessment of the performance of a registered service provider is to be by reference to whatever indicators of quality the Commission devises.

(4) The Commission must prepare a statement—

(a) setting out the frequency with which reviews under this section are to be conducted and the period to which they are to relate, and

(b) describing the method that it proposes to use in assessing and evaluating the performance of a registered service provider under this section.

(5) The Commission may—

(a) use different indicators for different cases,

(b) make different provision about frequency and period of reviews for different cases, and

(c) describe different methods for different cases.

(6) The Commission must publish—

(a) any indicators it devises for the purpose of subsection (3), and

(b) the statement it prepares for the purpose of subsection (4).

(7) Before doing so, the Commission—

(a) must consult the Secretary of State and such other persons, or other persons of such a description, as may be prescribed, and

(b) may also consult any other persons it considers appropriate.

(8) The Commission may from time to time revise—

(a) any indicators it devises for the purpose of subsection (3), and

(b) the statement it prepares for the purpose of subsection (4);

and, if it does so, it must publish the indicators and statement as revised.

(9) Subsection (7) applies to revised indicators and a revised statement, so far as the Commission considers the revisions in question to be significant.

(10) In this section "registered service provider" means a person registered under Chapter 2 as a service provider.

(11) Consultation undertaken before the commencement of this section is as effective for the purposes of subsection (7) as consultation undertaken after that commencement."

(3) Sections 47 (frequency and period of reviews under section 46) and 49 (power to extend periodic review function) are repealed.

(4) In section 48 (special reviews and investigations), in subsection (1)—

(a) omit ", with the approval of the Secretary of State,", and

(b) at the end insert "; but the Commission may not conduct a review or investigation under subsection (2)(ba) or (bb) without the approval of the Secretary of State."

(5) Omit subsection (1A) of that section.

(6) In subsection (2) of that section, for "a periodic review" substitute "a review under section 46".

(7) In that subsection, after paragraph (ba) (but before the following "or") insert—

"(bb) the exercise of the functions of English local authorities in arranging for the provision of adult social services,".

(8) After subsection (3) of that section insert—

"(3A) A review or investigation under subsection (2)(b), in so far as it involves a review or investigation into the arrangements made for the provision of the adult social services in question, is to be treated as a review under subsection (2)(bb) (and the requirement for approval under subsection (1) is accordingly to apply)."

(9) In consequence of the preceding provisions of this section—

(a) in section 50(1) of the Health and Social Care Act 2008 (failings by English local authorities), omit "or 49";

(b) in section 51(1) of that Act (failings by Welsh NHS bodies), omit "or 49";

(c) in section 70(3)(a) of that Act (provision by Commission to Monitor of material relevant to review under section 46 or 49), omit "or 49";

(d) in section 72(a) of that Act (provision by Commission to Comptroller and Auditor General of material relevant to review under section 46 or 49), omit "or 49";

(e) in section 293 of the Health and Social Care Act 2012, omit subsections (1) and (2);

(f) in Schedule 5 to that Act (amendments in consequence of Part 1 of that Act), omit paragraphs 157, 159, 163 and 164.

False or misleading information

92 Offence

(1) A care provider of a specified description commits an offence if—

(a) it supplies, publishes or otherwise makes available information of a specified description,

(b) the supply, publication or making available by other means of information of that description is required under an enactment or other legal obligation, and

(c) the information is false or misleading in a material respect.

(2) But it is a defence for a care provider to prove that it took all reasonable steps and exercised all due diligence to prevent the provision of false or misleading information as mentioned in subsection (1).

(3) "Care provider" means—

(a) a public body which provides health services or adult social care in England,

(b) a person who provides health services or adult social care in England pursuant to arrangements made with a public body exercising functions in connection with the provision of such services or care, or

(c) a person who provides health services or adult social care in England all or part of the cost of which is paid for by means of a direct payment under section 12A of the National Health Service Act 2006 or under Part 1 of this Act.

(4) "Health services" means services which must or may be provided as part of the health service.

(5) "Adult social care"—

(a) includes all forms of personal care and other practical assistance for individuals who, by reason of age, illness, disability, pregnancy, childbirth, dependence on alcohol or drugs, or any other similar circumstances, are in need of such care or other assistance, but

(b) does not include anything provided by an establishment or agency for which Her Majesty's Chief Inspector of Education, Children's Services and Skills is the registration authority under section 5 of the Care Standards Act 2000.

(6) "Specified" means specified in regulations.

(7) If a care provider commits an offence under either of the provisions mentioned in subsection (8) in respect of the provision of information, the provision of that information by that provider does not also constitute an offence under subsection (1).

(8) The provisions referred to in subsection (7) are—

(a) section 44 of the Competition Act 1998 (provision of false or misleading information) as applied by section 72 of the Health and Social Care Act 2012 (functions of the OFT under Part 1 of the Competition Act 1998 to be concurrent functions of Monitor), and

(b) section 117 of the Enterprise Act 2002 (provision of false or misleading information) as applied by section 73 of the Health and Social Care Act 2012 (functions of the OFT under Part 4 of the Enterprise Act 2002 to be concurrent functions of Monitor).

(9) If a care provider commits an offence under subsection (1) in respect of the provision of information, the provision of that information by that provider does not also constitute an offence under section 64 of the Health and Social Care Act 2008 (failure to comply with request to provide information).

93 Penalties

(1) A person who is guilty of an offence under section 92 is liable—

(a) on summary conviction, to a fine;

(b) on conviction on indictment, to imprisonment for not more than two years or a fine (or both).

(2) A court before which a care provider is convicted of an offence under section 92 may (whether instead of or as well as imposing a fine under subsection (1)) make either or both of the following orders—

(a) a remedial order,

(b) a publicity order.

(3) A "remedial order" is an order requiring the care provider to take specified steps to remedy one or more of the following—

(a) the conduct specified in section 92(1),

(b) any matter that appears to the court to have resulted from the conduct,

(c) any deficiency, as regards the management of information, in the care provider's policies, systems or practices of which the conduct appears to the court to be an indication.

(4) A "publicity order" is an order requiring the care provider to publicise in a specified manner—

(a) the fact that it has been convicted of an offence under section 92,

(b) specified particulars of the offence,

(c) the amount of any fine imposed, and

(d) the terms of any remedial order made.

(5) A remedial order may be made only on an application by the prosecution specifying the terms of the proposed order; and any such order must be on such terms (whether those proposed or others) as the court considers appropriate having regard to any representations made, and any evidence adduced, in relation to that matter by the prosecution or on behalf of the care provider.

(6) A remedial order must specify a period within which the steps referred to in subsection (3) are to be taken.

(7) A publicity order must specify a period within which the requirements referred to in subsection (4) are to be complied with.

(8) A care provider that fails to comply with a remedial order or a publicity order commits an offence and is liable on conviction on indictment to a fine.

94 Offences by bodies

(1) Subsection (2) applies where an offence under section 92(1) is committed by a body corporate and it is proved that the offence is committed by, or with the consent or connivance of, or is attributable to neglect on the part of—

(a) a director, manager or secretary of the body, or

(b) a person purporting to act in such a capacity.

(2) The director, manager, secretary or person purporting to act as such (as well as the body) is guilty of the offence and liable to be proceeded against and punished accordingly (but section 93(2) does not apply).

(3) The reference in subsection (2) to a director, manager or secretary of a body corporate includes a reference—

(a) to any other similar officer of the body, and

(b) where the body is a local authority, to a member of the authority.

(4) Proceedings for an offence under section 92(1) alleged to have been committed by an unincorporated association are to be brought in the name of the association (and not in that of any of the members); and rules of court relating to the service of documents have effect as if the unincorporated association were a body corporate.

(5) In proceedings for an offence under section 92(1) brought against an unincorporated association, section 33 of the Criminal Justice Act 1925 and Schedule 3 to the Magistrates' Courts Act 1980 apply as they apply in relation to a body corporate.

(6) A fine imposed on an unincorporated association on its conviction for an offence under section 92(1) is to be paid out of the funds of the association.

(7) Subsection (8) applies if an offence under section 92(1) is proved—

(a) to have been committed by, or with the consent or connivance of, an officer of the association or a member of its governing body, or

(b) to be attributable to neglect on the part of such an officer or member.

(8) The officer or member (as well as the association) is guilty of the offence and liable to be proceeded against accordingly (but section 93(2) does not apply).

Regulated activities

95 Training for persons working in regulated activity

In section 20 of the Health and Social Care Act 2008 (regulation of regulated activities), after subsection (4) insert—

"(4A) Regulations made under this section by virtue of subsection (3)(d) may in particular include provision for a specified person to set the standards which persons undergoing the training in question must attain."

PART 3

HEALTH

CHAPTER 1

HEALTH EDUCATION ENGLAND

Establishment

96 Health Education England

(1) There is to be a body corporate called Health Education England (referred to in this Act as "HEE").

(2) Schedule 5 (which includes provision about HEE's constitution, the exercise of its functions and its financial and reporting duties) has effect.

(3) The Special Health Authority called Health Education England is abolished; and, in consequence of that, the following are revoked—

- (a) the Health Education England (Establishment and Constitution) Order 2012 (S.I. 2012/1273), and
- (b) the Health Education England Regulations (S.I. 2012/1290).

(4) The Secretary of State may by order provide for the transfer of property, rights and liabilities from that Special Health Authority to HEE; for further provision about an order under this section, see section 118.

National functions

97 Planning education and training for health care workers etc.

(1) HEE must perform on behalf of the Secretary of State the duty under section 1F(1) of the National Health Service Act 2006 (planning and delivery of education and training), so far as that duty applies to the functions of the Secretary of State under—

- (a) section 63(1) and (5) of the Health Services and Public Health Act 1968 (instruction for officers of hospital authorities etc.),
- (b) section 258(1) of the National Health Service Act 2006 (university clinical teaching and research), and

(c) such other of the enactments listed in section 1F(3) of that Act as regulations may specify.

(2) Regulations may—

(a) provide for the duty under section 1F(1) of the National Health Service Act 2006 to apply to such other functions of the Secretary of State as are specified; and

(b) impose on HEE a duty to perform the duty as it applies as a result of provision made under paragraph (a).

(3) Regulations may provide that the duty under subsection (1) or a duty imposed under subsection (2) may only be performed, or may not be performed, in relation to persons of a specified description.

(4) In each of the following provisions of the National Health Service Act 2006, after "the Secretary of State" insert "and Health Education England"—

(a) section 1F(2) (duty on providers of health services to support system of education and training for health care workers);

(b) section 13M (duty on National Health Service Commissioning Board to support that system);

(c) section 14Z (duty on clinical commissioning groups to support that system).

(5) Regulations may give HEE further functions relating to education and training for health care workers.

(6) HEE may, with the consent of the Secretary of State, carry out other activities relating to—

(a) education and training for health care workers;

(b) the provision of information and advice on careers in the health service.

(7) After section 63(6) of the Health Services and Public Health Act 1968 insert—

"(6A) The Secretary of State may make such other payments as the Secretary of State considers appropriate to persons availing themselves of such instruction in England.

(6B) The Secretary of State may make a payment under subsection (6)(b) or (6A) subject to such terms and conditions as the Secretary of State decides; and the Secretary of State's power to make such a payment includes power to suspend or terminate the payment, or to require repayment, in such circumstances as the Secretary of State decides."

(8) The power of the Secretary of State under section 63(6) or (6A) of the Health Services and Public Health Act 1968 is exercisable concurrently with HEE; but, in exercising the power, HEE must have regard to any guidance or other information issued by the Secretary of State about its exercise.

(9) "Health care workers" means persons in relation to whom HEE's duty under section 1F(1) of the National Health Service Act 2006 is to be performed.

98 Ensuring sufficient skilled health care workers for the health service

(1) HEE must exercise its functions with a view to ensuring that a sufficient number of persons with the skills and training to work as health care workers for the purposes of the health service is available to do so throughout England.

(2) Regulations may provide that the duty under subsection (1) may only be performed, or may not be performed, in relation to persons of a specified description.

99 Quality improvement in education and training, etc.

(1) HEE must exercise its functions with a view to securing continuous improvement—

(a) in the quality of education and training provided for health care workers;

(b) in the quality of health services.

(2) HEE must, in exercising its functions, promote—

(a) research into matters relating to such of the activities listed in section 63(2) of the Health Services and Public Health Act 1968 (social care services, primary care services and other health services) as are relevant to HEE's functions, and

(b) the use in those activities of evidence obtained from the research.

(3) In section 2(2) of the Health Act 2009 (bodies required to have regard to NHS Constitution when exercising health service functions), after paragraph (g) insert—

"(h) Health Education England."

(4) HEE must exercise its functions with a view to securing that education and training for health care workers is provided in a way which promotes the NHS Constitution.

(5) "Health services" means health services provided as part of the health service.

(6) "NHS Constitution" has the meaning given by section 1(1) of the Health Act 2009.

100 Objectives, priorities and outcomes

(1) The Secretary of State must publish before the start of each financial year a document which specifies the objectives and priorities that the Secretary of State has set for HEE for that year in relation to the education and training to be provided for health care workers.

(2) The Secretary of State must also publish at intervals of not more than three years a document (called the "Education Outcomes Framework") which specifies the outcomes that the Secretary of State has set for HEE to achieve having regard to those objectives and priorities.

(3) The Secretary of State—

(a) may revise a document published under subsection (1) or (2), and

(b) if the Secretary of State does so, must publish it as revised.

(4) HEE must publish a document which—

(a) specifies the objectives and priorities that it has set, for the period specified in the document, for the planning and delivery of education and training to health care workers,

(b) specifies the outcomes that HEE expects to achieve in that respect during that period having regard to those objectives and priorities, and

(c) includes, or refers to a document which includes, guidance for LETBs (see section 103) on the exercise of the function under section 107(1).

(5) In performing the duty under subsection (4), HEE must have regard, in particular, to its objectives in the longer term in relation to the planning and delivery of education and training to health care workers.

(6) HEE must ensure that the objectives, priorities and outcomes specified for the purposes of subsection (4)(a) and (b) are consistent with those specified for the purposes of subsections (1) and (2).

(7) A document under subsection (4) may specify different periods in relation to different categories of health care worker.

(8) HEE must, before the end of 12 months beginning with the date on which a document under subsection (4) is published—

(a) review the document, and,

(b) if HEE revises it, publish it as revised.

(9) HEE may perform the duty under subsection (4) by publishing two or more documents which, taken together, comply with that subsection.

(10) HEE must seek to achieve the objectives and outcomes and to reflect the priorities specified in any document—

(a) published by the Secretary of State under subsection (1), (2) or (3);

(b) published by HEE under subsection (4) or (8).

101 Sections 98 and 100: matters to which HEE must have regard

(1) In performing the duty under section 98(1) (ensuring sufficient skilled workers for the health service) or the duty under section 100(4) (setting objectives, priorities and outcomes for education and training), HEE must have regard to the following matters in particular—

(a) the likely future demand for health services and for persons with the skills and training to work as health care workers for the purposes of the health service,

(b) the sustainability of the supply of persons with the skills and training to work as such,

(c) the priorities that providers of health services have for the education and training of persons wishing to work as such,

(d) the mandate published under section 13A of the National Health Service Act 2006,

(e) the objectives of the Secretary of State in exercising public health functions (as defined by section 1H of that Act),

(f) the priorities that the National Health Service Commissioning Board has for the provision of health services,

(g) documents published by the Secretary of State under section 100(1), (2) or (3),

(h) the desirability of promoting the integration of health provision with health-related provision and care and support provision,

(i) the desirability of enabling health care workers to switch between different posts relating to health provision, health-related provision or care and support provision, and

(j) such other matters as regulations may specify.

(2) In subsection (1), "health provision", "health-related provision" and "care and support provision" each have the same meaning as in section 3.

102 Advice

(1) HEE must make arrangements for obtaining advice on the exercise of its functions from persons who are involved in, or who HEE thinks otherwise have an interest in, the provision of education and training for health care workers.

(2) HEE must seek to ensure that it receives representations from the following, in particular, under the arrangements it makes under subsection (1)—

(a) persons who provide health services;
(b) persons to whom health services are provided;
(c) carers for persons to whom health services are provided;
(d) health care workers;
(e) bodies which regulate health care workers;
(f) persons who provide, or contribute to the provision of, education and training for health care workers.

(3) HEE may perform a duty under subsection (2) by seeking to ensure that it receives representations from organisations which represent the persons referred to in the paragraph in question.

(4) HEE must advise the Secretary of State on such matters relating to its functions as the Secretary of State may request; and a request under this subsection may specify how and when the advice is to be provided.

(5) "Carer" means an adult who provides or intends to provide care for another person.

Local functions

103 Local Education and Training Boards

(1) HEE must, in exercise of the power under paragraph 9 of Schedule 5, appoint committees for areas in England, each of which is to be called a Local Education and Training Board (referred to in this Chapter as an "LETB").

(2) The main function of an LETB is to exercise on HEE's behalf its functions under sections 97(1) and 98(1) (planning and delivering education for health care workers and ensuring sufficient skilled health care workers in the health service), so far as they are exercisable in or in relation to the LETB's area.

(3) In carrying out its main function, an LETB must represent the interests of all the persons who provide health services in the area for which the LETB is appointed.

(4) Subsections (1), (2) and (4) of section 99 (quality improvement in education and training etc.) apply to an LETB in the exercise of its functions as they apply to HEE in the exercise of its functions.

(5) An LETB may co-operate with another LETB in the exercise of functions; and two or more LETBs may exercise functions jointly.

(6) HEE may attend any meeting held by an LETB about a matter of concern to HEE.

104 LETBs: appointment etc.

(1) Where, on an application under this section, HEE is satisfied that the applicants meet the criteria that HEE has set for the purpose (the "appointment criteria"), HEE must appoint the applicants as members of an LETB for such area as HEE considers appropriate.

(2) Where, on an application under this section, HEE is satisfied that the applicants meet some (but not all) of the appointment criteria, it may nonetheless appoint the applicants as the members of an LETB for such area and subject to such conditions as HEE considers appropriate.

(3) The members of an LETB must include—
- (a) persons who provide health services in the area for which the LETB is appointed,
- (b) persons who have clinical expertise of a description specified in regulations, and
- (c) a person who will represent the interests of patients.

(4) Regulations under paragraph (b) of subsection (3) may require a specified number of members to have the expertise mentioned in that paragraph.

(5) The following persons are also eligible to be appointed as members of an LETB—
- (a) persons who, in the area for which the LETB is appointed, provide education or training for health care workers or for persons wishing to work as health care workers, and
- (b) persons of such other description as HEE may decide.

(6) A member of HEE is not eligible for membership of an LETB.

(7) The appointment criteria must include criteria designed to ensure that a majority of the members of an LETB are persons who provide health services in the area for which the LETB in question is appointed.

(8) If HEE is unable (for reasons beyond its control) to comply with any requirement imposed by this section or regulations under this section to appoint persons of a particular description as members of an LETB, HEE may instead appoint employees of HEE (other than members of HEE).

(9) On appointing an LETB, HEE must appoint the chair of the LETB; but it may not appoint as chair a person who—
- (a) provides health services in the area for which the LETB is appointed, or
- (b) in the area for which the LETB is appointed, provides education or training for health care workers or for persons wishing to work as health care workers.

(10) HEE must notify applicants under subsection (1) or (2) of the decision on the application and—
- (a) in the case of an approval of such an application, the area for which the LETB is appointed and the appointment under subsection (9);
- (b) in the case of a rejection, the reasons for the rejection.

(11) HEE, having complied with subsection (10), must publish—
- (a) the decision, and
- (b) in the case of a rejection, the reasons for the rejection.

(12) The conditions on which a person is appointed as a member of an LETB must include a condition not to use information obtained in the capacity as such otherwise than for the purposes of the LETB.

(13) Regulations may make further provision about—

(a) the membership of an LETB;

(b) the removal by HEE of members of an LETB;

(c) the suspension by HEE of members of an LETB.

(14) Schedule 6 (which includes provision about the area of an LETB, the appointment criteria and the exercise of an LETB's functions) has effect.

105 LETBs: co-operation by providers of health services

(1) Regulations must require specified commissioners of health services to include in the arrangements under the National Health Service Act 2006 for the provision of such services terms to ensure that a provider of such services—

(a) co-operates with the LETB for each area in which it provides such services, in such manner and to such extent as the LETB in question may request, in planning the provision of, and in providing, education and training for health care workers;

(b) provides the LETB in question with such information as it may request;

(c) complies with such other obligations relating to education and training for health care workers as may be specified.

(2) Duties imposed by regulations under subsection (1) on commissioners of health services are in addition to the duty imposed on such persons by section 1F(2) of the National Health Service Act 2006 (duty to secure that persons providing health services co-operate with the Secretary of State in the discharge of the duty as to education and training).

(3) Regulations may specify factors to which an LETB must, when proposing to make a request of the type mentioned in subsection (1)(a) or (b), have regard in considering the reasonableness of making the request.

(4) A reference to a commissioner of health services is a reference to—

(a) the National Health Service Commissioning Board,

(b) a clinical commissioning group, or

(c) such other person as arranges for the provision of such services.

106 Education and training plans

(1) An LETB must publish for each financial year a document (called an "education and training plan") specifying how it proposes to exercise its main function (see section 103(2)).

(2) The education and training plan of an LETB must specify how the LETB proposes to—

(a) achieve the objectives and reflect the priorities set by the Secretary of State for the purposes of section 100(1),

(b) achieve the objectives and reflect the priorities set by HEE for the purposes of section 100(4)(a),

(c) achieve the outcomes set by the Secretary of State for the purposes of section 100(2), and

(d) achieve the outcomes set by HEE for the purposes of section 100(4)(b).

(3) In preparing its education and training plan, an LETB must have regard to—

(a) the priorities that the providers of health services whom the LETB represents have in relation to the provision in the LETB's area of health services and of education and training for health care workers or persons wishing to become health care workers,

(b) the priorities that commissioners of health services in the LETB's area have in relation to those matters,

(c) any assessment of relevant needs relating to the LETB's area prepared under section 116 of the Local Government and Public Involvement in Health Act 2007,

(d) any joint health and wellbeing strategy relating to the LETB's area prepared under section 116A of that Act, and

(e) the LETB's objectives in the longer term in relation to the exercise of the LETB's main function.

(4) In preparing its education and training plan, an LETB must involve—

(a) the providers of health services whom the LETB represents,

(b) the commissioners of health services in the LETB's area,

(c) the Health and Wellbeing Board for that area,

(d) such persons as HEE may direct the LETB to involve, and

(e) such other persons as the LETB considers appropriate.

(5) Before publishing its education and training plan (or an amended education and training plan), an LETB must obtain approval of the plan (or the amended plan) from HEE.

(6) Before giving an approval under subsection (5), HEE may direct the LETB concerned to amend the education and training plan (or the amended education and training plan) as HEE specifies.

(7) But, in the case of an LETB which meets all the appointment criteria, the only amendments which HEE may direct to be made under subsection (6) are those HEE considers necessary in order to ensure that the LETB achieves the outcomes set by HEE for the purposes of section 100(4)(b).

(8) Where HEE exercises the power under subsection (6), it must publish—

(a) the amendments in question, and

(b) its reasons for directing them to be made.

(9) HEE may give LETBs directions about—

(a) what to include in their education and training plans;

(b) how to present them.

(10) An LETB may perform the duty under subsection (1) by preparing two or more documents which, taken together, specify how it proposes to exercise its main function.

107 Commissioning education and training

(1) Each LETB must for each financial year arrange for the provision of education and training in accordance with its education and training plan for that year.

(2) Where HEE considers that it would be better for the arrangements for the provision of certain education and training to be made on a national basis, it—

(a) may arrange for the provision of that education and training accordingly, or

(b) may direct one or more LETBs to do so on its behalf.

(3) Before exercising a power under subsection (2), HEE must involve LETBs in making its decision.

(4) HEE must for each financial year allocate to each LETB the amount that HEE considers appropriate to enable the LETB to comply with this section.

(5) In doing so, HEE must take into account any duty to which the LETB is subject under section 108(9) (requirement to make payments by reference to an approved tariff price or a price varied under a specified procedure).

(6) An LETB may arrange for another person to help it to exercise the function under subsection (1) or (where it is directed to do so under subsection (2)(b)) the function under subsection (2)(a) (and such functions as are exercisable for the purposes of or in connection with the exercise of the function concerned).

(7) Each LETB—

(a) must keep under review the quality of the education and training the provision of which it arranges, and

(b) must report its findings to such persons as it considers may be interested by them.

(8) An LETB must produce such reports on the exercise of the function under subsection (1) (including on the quality of the education and training the provision of which it arranges) as HEE may require.

Tariffs

108 Tariffs

(1) The Secretary of State may specify a tariff setting approved prices in respect of education and training.

(2) The approved prices may be different for different descriptions of education and training (and may in particular be different for different areas).

(3) A tariff specified under subsection (1) must be published.

(4) If a tariff is specified under subsection (1), the Secretary of State may also specify a procedure for varying the approved prices in particular cases or descriptions of cases.

(5) If the Secretary of State does so, the procedure—

(a) must be published, and

(b) must require a price as varied under the procedure to be published.

(6) A published tariff or variation procedure may be revised or revoked by the Secretary of State.

(7) If a tariff or variation procedure is revised, the Secretary of State must publish it as revised.

(8) If it is revoked, the Secretary of State must publish a statement to that effect.

(9) Where a tariff sets an approved price for a particular description of education or training, payments made by an LETB or HEE in respect of the provision of that description of education or training must be made—

(a) by reference to the approved price, or

(b) where the approved price has been varied in accordance with a variation procedure that has effect in relation to it, by reference to the price as varied.

CHAPTER 2

HEALTH RESEARCH AUTHORITY

Establishment

109 The Health Research Authority

(1) There is to be a body corporate called the Health Research Authority (referred to in this Act as "the HRA").

(2) Schedule 7 (which includes provision about the HRA's constitution, the exercise of its functions and its financial and reporting duties) has effect.

(3) The Special Health Authority called the Health Research Authority is abolished; and, in consequence of that, the following are revoked—

(a) the Health Research Authority (Establishment and Constitution) Order 2011 (S.I. 2011/2323), and

(b) the Health Research Authority Regulations 2011 (S.I. 2011/2341).

(4) The Secretary of State may by order provide for the transfer of property, rights and liabilities from that Special Health Authority to the HRA; for further provision about an order under this section, see section 118.

General functions

110 The HRA's functions

(1) The main functions of the HRA are—

(a) functions relating to the co-ordination and standardisation of practice relating to the regulation of health and social care research (see section 111);

(b) functions relating to research ethics committees (see sections 112 to 115);

(c) functions as a member of the United Kingdom Ethics Committee Authority (see section 116 and the Medicines for Human Use (Clinical Trials) Regulations 2004 (S.I. 2004/1031));

(d) functions relating to approvals for processing confidential information relating to patients (see section 117 and the Health Service (Control of Patient Information) Regulations 2002 (S.I. 2002/1438)).

(2) The main objective of the HRA in exercising its functions is—

(a) to protect participants and potential participants in health or social care research and the general public by encouraging research that is safe and ethical, and

(b) to promote the interests of those participants and potential participants and the general public by facilitating the conduct of research that is safe and ethical (including by promoting transparency in research).

(3) Health research is research into matters relating to people's physical or mental health; but a reference to health research does not include a reference to anything authorised under the Animals (Scientific Procedures) Act 1986.

(4) Social care research is research into matters relating to personal care or other practical assistance for individuals aged 18 or over who are in need of care or assistance because of age, physical or mental illness, disability, pregnancy, childbirth, dependence on alcohol or drugs or other similar circumstances; and "illness" has the meaning given by section 275(1) of the National Health Service Act 2006.

(5) A reference to health or social care research does not include a reference to research into matters which are within the legislative competence of a devolved legislature.

(6) A reference to research that is ethical is a reference to research that conforms to generally accepted ethical standards.

(7) Promoting transparency in research includes promoting—

(a) the registration of research;

(b) the publication and dissemination of research findings and conclusions;

(c) the provision of access to data on which research findings or conclusions are based;

(d) the provision of information at the end of research to participants in the research;

(e) the provision of access to tissue used in research, for use in future research.

(8) The Secretary of State may by order amend subsection (1) in consequence of—

(a) functions being given to the HRA,

(b) functions being taken away from the HRA, or

(c) changes to the description of functions that the HRA has for the time being.

Regulatory practice

111 Co-ordinating and promoting regulatory practice etc.

(1) The HRA and each of the following must co-operate with each other in the exercise of their respective functions relating to health or social care research, with a view to co-ordinating and standardising practice relating to the regulation of such research—

(a) the Secretary of State;

(b) the licensing authority for the purposes of the Medicines Act 1968;

(c) the Health and Social Care Information Centre;

(d) the Chief Medical Officer of the Department of Health;
(e) the Human Fertilisation and Embryology Authority;
(f) the Human Tissue Authority;
(g) the Care Quality Commission;
(h) the Administration of Radioactive Substances Advisory Committee;
(i) such person, or a person of such description, as regulations may specify.

(2) In performing the duty under subsection (1), a person must have regard to the need—

(a) to protect participants and potential participants in health or social care research and the general public by encouraging research that is safe and ethical, and
(b) to promote the interests of those participants and potential participants and the general public by facilitating the conduct of such research.

(3) The HRA must promote the co-ordination and standardisation of practice in the United Kingdom relating to the regulation of health and social care research; and it must, in doing so, seek to ensure that such regulation is proportionate.

(4) The HRA and each devolved authority must co-operate with each other in the exercise of their respective functions relating to the regulation of assessments of the ethics of health and social care research, with a view to co-ordinating and standardising practice in the United Kingdom relating to such regulation.

(5) The HRA must—

(a) keep under review matters relating to the ethics of health or social care research and matters relating to the regulation of such research, and
(b) provide the Secretary of State with such advice about the matters referred to in paragraph (a) as the Secretary of State requests.

(6) The HRA must publish guidance on—

(a) principles of good practice in the management and conduct of health and social care research;
(b) requirements, whether imposed by enactments or otherwise, to which persons conducting health or social care research are subject.

(7) A local authority (within the meaning of Part 1), an NHS trust established under section 25 of the National Health Service Act 2006 and an NHS foundation trust must each have regard to guidance under subsection (6).

(8) The ways in which persons may co-operate with each other under subsection (1) or (4) include, for example, by sharing information.

(9) Section 290 of the Health and Social Care Act 2012 (duties for health and social care authorities to co-operate), so far as applying to a person who is for the time being within subsection (1), does not apply to functions of that person relating to health or social care research.

(10) Section 110(5) (exclusion of research into matters within devolved competence) does not apply to the reference in subsection (1) or (4) to health and social care research.

Research ethics committees

112 The HRA's policy on research ethics committees

(1) The HRA must ensure that research ethics committees it recognises or establishes under this Chapter provide an efficient and effective means of assessing the ethics of health and social care research.

(2) A research ethics committee is a group of persons which assesses the ethics of research involving individuals; and the ways in which health or social care research might involve individuals include, for example—

(a) by obtaining information from them;

(b) by obtaining bodily tissue or fluid from them;

(c) by using information, tissue or fluid obtained from them on a previous occasion;

(d) by requiring them to undergo a test or other process (including xenotransplantation).

(3) For the purposes of subsection (1), the HRA—

(a) must publish a document (called "the REC policy document") which specifies the requirements which it expects research ethics committees it recognises or establishes under this Chapter to comply with, and

(b) must monitor their compliance with those requirements.

(4) The HRA may do such other things in relation to research ethics committees it recognises or establishes under this Chapter as it considers appropriate; it may, for example—

(a) co-ordinate their work;

(b) allocate work to them;

(c) develop and maintain training programmes designed to ensure that their members and staff can carry out their work effectively;

(d) provide them with advice and help (including help in the form of financial assistance).

(5) The requirements in the REC policy document may, for example, relate to—

(a) membership;

(b) proceedings;

(c) staff;

(d) accommodation and facilities;

(e) expenses;

(f) objectives and functions;

(g) accountability;

(h) procedures for challenging decisions.

(6) The HRA must ensure that the requirements imposed on research ethics committees in the REC policy document do not conflict with the requirements imposed on them by the Medicines for Human Use (Clinical Trials) Regulations 2004 (S.I. 2004/1031).

(7) Before publishing the REC policy document, the HRA must consult—

(a) the devolved authorities, and

(b) such other persons as it considers appropriate.

(8) The HRA may revise the REC policy document and, where it does so, it must publish the document as revised; subsection (7) applies to a revised policy document in so far as the HRA considers the revisions significant.

(9) The HRA must indemnify the members of each research ethics committee it recognises or establishes under this Chapter against any liability to a third party for loss, damage or injury arising from the committee's exercise of its functions in assessing the ethics of health or social care research.

113 Approval of research

(1) The HRA must publish guidance about—

(a) the cases in which, in its opinion, good practice requires a person proposing to conduct health or social care research that involves individuals to obtain the approval of a research ethics committee recognised or established by the HRA under this Chapter, and

(b) the cases in which an enactment requires a person proposing to conduct research of that kind to obtain that approval.

(2) Before publishing guidance under subsection (1), the HRA must—

(a) consult the devolved authorities and such other persons as the HRA considers appropriate, and

(b) obtain the approval of the Secretary of State.

(3) The HRA may revise guidance under subsection (1) and, where it does so, it must publish the guidance as revised; subsection (2) applies to revised guidance in so far as the HRA considers the revisions significant.

(4) Schedule 8 (which amends various references to research ethics committees in secondary legislation) has effect.

114 Recognition by the HRA

(1) The HRA may, on an application made by or on behalf of a group of persons, recognise the group as a research ethics committee which is capable of—

(a) approving research of the kind referred to in section 113(1), and

(b) giving such other approvals as enactments require.

(2) The HRA may not recognise a group under this section unless it is satisfied that—

(a) the group will, if recognised, comply with the requirements set out in the REC policy document, and

(b) there is or will be a demand for such a group.

(3) In deciding whether to recognise a group under this section, the HRA must have regard to whether the group is recognised as a research ethics committee by or on behalf of a devolved authority.

(4) The HRA may do anything (including providing financial assistance) to help a group wishing to be recognised under this section to reach a position from which it should be able to make an application for recognition under this section that is likely to succeed.

(5) The HRA may revoke a recognition under this section if it is satisfied that—

(a) the group to which the recognition applies is not complying with the requirements specified in the REC policy document,

(b) the group is not (or is not properly) carrying out its function of assessing the ethical aspects of research, or

(c) revocation is necessary or desirable for some other reason.

(6) A group in existence immediately before the commencement of section 109, and established or recognised by or on behalf of the old Health Research Authority, or by or on behalf of the Secretary of State, as a research ethics committee which assesses health or social care research is to be regarded as recognised by the HRA under this section.

(7) The reference in subsection (6) to the old Health Research Authority is a reference to the Special Health Authority called the Health Research Authority (and abolished by section 109).

115 Establishment by the HRA

(1) The HRA may establish research ethics committees which have the following functions—

(a) approving research of the kind referred to in section 113(1);

(b) giving such other approvals as enactments require.

(2) The HRA must ensure that a research ethics committee established under this section complies with the requirements set out in the REC policy document.

(3) The HRA may abolish a research ethics committee established under this section.

116 Membership of the United Kingdom Ethics Committee Authority

In regulation 5 of the Medicines for Human Use (Clinical Trials) Regulations 2004 (S.I. 2004/1031) (United Kingdom Ethics Committee Authority)—

(a) in paragraphs (1), (2) and (3), for "the Secretary of State for Health", in each place it appears, substitute "the Health Research Authority", and

(b) in paragraph (2), for "the Secretary of State" substitute "the Health Research Authority".

Patient information

117 Approval for processing confidential patient information

(1) The Health Service (Control of Patient Information) Regulations 2002 (S.I. 2002/1438) are amended as follows.

(2) In regulation 5 (the title to which becomes "Approval for processing information")—

(a) the existing text becomes paragraph (1), and

(b) in sub-paragraph (a) of that paragraph, for "both the Secretary of State and a research ethics committee" substitute "the Health Research Authority".

(3) After paragraph (1) of that regulation insert—

"(2) The Health Research Authority may not give an approval under paragraph (1)(a) unless a research ethics committee has approved the medical research concerned."

(4) After paragraph (2) of that regulation insert—

"(3) The Health Research Authority shall put in place and operate a system for reviewing decisions it makes under paragraph (1)(a)."

(5) In regulation 6 (registration requirements in relation to information), in paragraph (1)—

(a) before "the Secretary of State" insert "the Health Research Authority or", and

(b) before "he" insert "it or".

(6) In paragraph (2)(d) of that regulation, before "the Secretary of State" insert "the Health Research Authority or (as the case may be)".

(7) In paragraph (3) of that regulation, for the words from the beginning to "in the register" substitute "The Health Research Authority shall retain the particulars of each entry it records in the register, and the Secretary of State shall retain the particulars of each entry he records in the register,".

(8) For paragraph (4) of that regulation substitute—

"(4) The Health Research Authority shall, in such manner and to such extent as it considers appropriate, publish entries it records in the register; and the Secretary of State shall, in such manner and to such extent as he considers appropriate, publish entries he records in the register."

CHAPTER 3

CHAPTERS 1 AND 2: SUPPLEMENTARY

Miscellaneous

118 Transfer orders

(1) An order under section 96 (establishment of Health Education England) or section 109 (establishment of the Health Research Authority) (a "transfer order") may make provision for rights and liabilities relating to an individual's contract of employment.

(2) A transfer order may, in particular, make provision the same as or similar to provision in the Transfer of Undertakings (Protection of Employment) Regulations 2006 (S.I. 2006/246).

(3) A transfer order may provide for the transfer of property, rights or liabilities—

(a) whether or not they would otherwise be capable of being transferred;

(b) irrespective of any requirement for consent that would otherwise apply.

(4) A transfer order may create rights, or impose liabilities, in relation to property, rights or liabilities transferred.

(5) A transfer order may provide for things done by or in relation to the transferor for the purposes of or in connection with anything transferred to be—

(a) treated as done by or in relation to the transferee or its employees;

(b) continued by or in relation to the transferee or its employees.

(6) A transfer order may in particular make provision about continuation of legal proceedings.

General

119 Chapters 1 and 2: interpretation and supplementary provision

(1) For the purposes of Chapters 1 and 2, an expression in the first column of the following table is defined or otherwise explained by the provision of this Act specified in the second column.

Expression	*Provision*
Appointment criteria	Section 104
Commissioner of health services	Section 105
Devolved authority	Section 126
Devolved legislature	Section 126
Direct or direction	Subsection (2) below
Enactment	Section 126
Financial year	Section 126
Health care workers	Section 97
Health research	Section 110
The health service	Section 126
Health services	Section 99
HEE	Section 96
The HRA	Section 109
LETB	Section 103
Social care research	Section 110

(2) A power under Chapter 1 or 2 to give a direction—

(a) includes a power to vary or revoke the direction by a subsequent direction, and

(b) must be exercised by giving the direction in question in writing.

(3) The amendments made by sections 116 and 117 and Schedule 8 to provisions of subordinate legislation do not affect the power to make further subordinate legislation amending or revoking the amended provisions.

CHAPTER 4

TRUST SPECIAL ADMINISTRATION

120 Powers of administrator etc.

(1) In section 65O of the National Health Service Act 2006 (Chapter 5A of Part 2: interpretation) (the existing text of which becomes subsection (1)) at the end insert—

"(2) The references in this Chapter to taking action in relation to an NHS trust include a reference to taking action, including in relation to another NHS trust or an NHS foundation trust, which is necessary for and consequential on action taken in relation to that NHS trust.

(3) The references in this Chapter to taking action in relation to an NHS foundation trust include a reference to taking action, including in relation to another NHS foundation trust or an NHS trust, which is necessary for and consequential on action taken in relation to that NHS foundation trust."

(2) In section 65F of that Act (administrator's draft report), in subsection (1), for "45 working days" substitute "65 working days".

(3) In subsection (5)(a) of that section, for "would achieve the objective set out in section 65DA(1)(a)" substitute "—

(i) would achieve the objective set out in section 65DA(1)(a), and

(ii) would do so without harming essential services provided for the purposes of the NHS by any other NHS foundation trust or NHS trust that provides services under this Act to the commissioner,".

(4) After subsection (7) of that section insert—

"(8) Where the administrator recommends taking action in relation to another NHS foundation trust or an NHS trust, the references in subsection (5) to a commissioner also include a reference to a person to which the other NHS foundation trust or the NHS trust provides services under this Act that would be affected by the action.

(9) A service provided by an NHS foundation trust or an NHS trust is an essential service for the purposes of subsection (5) if the person making the statement in question is satisfied that the criterion in section 65DA(3) is met.

(10) Section 65DA(4) applies to the person making the statement when that person is determining whether that criterion is met."

(5) In section 65G of that Act (consultation plan), in subsection (2), for "30 working days" substitute "40 working days".

(6) In subsection (4)(a) of that section, for "would achieve the objective set out in section 65DA(1)(a)" substitute "—

(i) would achieve the objective set out in section 65DA(1)(a), and

(ii) would do so without harming essential services provided for the purposes of the NHS by any other NHS foundation trust or NHS trust that provides services under this Act to the commissioner,".

(7) After subsection (6) of that section insert—

"(7) Where the administrator recommends taking action in relation to another NHS foundation trust or an NHS trust, the references in subsection (4) to a commissioner also include a reference to a person to which the other NHS foundation trust or the NHS trust provides services under this Act that would be affected by the action."

(8) A service provided by an NHS foundation trust or an NHS trust is an essential service for the purposes of subsection (4) if the person making the statement in question is satisfied that the criterion in section 65DA(3) is met.

(9) Section 65DA(4) applies to the person making the statement when that person is determining whether that criterion is met."

(8) In section 65H of that Act (consultation requirements), in subsection (4)—

(a) after "trust special administrator must" insert "—

(a)",

and

(b) at the end insert ", and

(b) in the case of each affected trust, hold at least one meeting to seek responses from staff of the trust and from such persons as the trust special administrator may recognise as representing staff of the trust."

(9) In subsection (7) of that section, after paragraph (b) (but before paragraph (ba) inserted by section 85(10)(a) of this Act) insert—

"(bza) any affected trust;

(bzb) any person to which an affected trust provides goods or services under this Act that would be affected by the action recommended in the draft report;

(bzc) any local authority in whose area the trust provides goods or services under this Act;

(bzd) any local authority in whose area an affected trust provides goods or services under this Act;

(bze) any Local Healthwatch organisation for the area of a local authority mentioned in paragraph (bzc) or (bzd);".

(10) In subsection (8) of that section, omit paragraph (e).

(11) In subsection (9) of that section—

(a) after "trust special administrator must" insert "—

(a)",

(b) after "subsection (7)(b)," (but before the insertion made by section 85(10)(b) of this Act) insert "(bzb),", and

(c) at the end insert—

"(b) hold at least one meeting to seek responses from representatives of each of the trusts from which the administrator must request a written response under subsection (7)(bza), and

(c) hold at least one meeting to seek responses from representatives of each of the local authorities and Local Healthwatch organisations from which the administrator must request a written response under subsection (7)(bzc), (bzd) and (bze)."

(12) After subsection (11) of that section, insert—

"(11A) In this section, "affected trust" means—

(a) where the trust in question is an NHS trust, another NHS trust, or an NHS foundation trust, which provides goods or services under this Act that would be affected by the action recommended in the draft report;

(b) where the trust in question is an NHS foundation trust, another NHS foundation trust, or an NHS trust, which provides services under this Act that would be affected by the action recommended in the draft report.

(11B) In this section, a reference to a local authority includes a reference to the council of a district only where the district is comprised in an area for which there is no county council."

(13) In subsection (12)(a) of that section, after "subsection (7)(b)", insert ", (bzb), (bzc) and (bzd)".

(14) In section 65N of that Act (guidance), after subsection (1) insert—

"(1A) It must, in so far as it applies to NHS trusts, include guidance about—

(a) seeking the support of commissioners for an administrator's recommendation;

(b) involving the Board in relation to finalising an administrator's report or draft report."

(15) In section 13Q of that Act (public involvement and consultation by NHS Commissioning Board), at the end insert—

"(4) This section does not require the Board to make arrangements in relation to matters to which a trust special administrator's report or draft report under section 65F or 65I relates before the Secretary of State makes a decision under section 65K(1), is satisfied as mentioned in section 65KB(1) or 65KD(1) or makes a decision under section 65KD(9) (as the case may be)."

(16) In section 14Z2 of that Act (public involvement and consultation by clinical commissioning groups), at the end insert—

"(7) This section does not require a clinical commissioning group to make arrangements in relation to matters to which a trust special administrator's report or draft report under section 65F or 65I relates before the Secretary of State makes a decision under section 65K(1), is satisfied as mentioned in section 65KB(1) or 65KD(1) or makes a decision under section 65KD(9) (as the case may be)."

(17) In section 242 of that Act (public involvement and consultation by NHS trusts and foundation trusts), in subsection (6)—

(a) for "65I, 65R or 65U" substitute "or 65I", and

(b) for the words from "the decision" to the end substitute "the Secretary of State makes a decision under section 65K(1), is satisfied as mentioned in section 65KB(1) or 65KD(1) or makes a decision under section 65KD(9) (as the case may be)."

(18) In Schedule 14 to the Health and Social Care Act 2012 (abolition of NHS trusts in England: consequential amendments)—

(a) after paragraph 4 insert—

"4A In section 13Q(4) (public involvement and consultation by Board), omit "makes a decision under section 65K(1),".

4B In section 14Z2 (public involvement and consultation by clinical commissioning groups), omit "makes a decision under section 65K(1),".",

(b) in paragraph 15(4), in the new subsection (2A) to be inserted into section 65F of the National Health Service Act 2006, in paragraph (a), for "would achieve the objective set out in section 65DA(1)(a)" substitute "—

(i) would achieve the objective set out in section 65DA(1)(a), and

(ii) would do so without harming essential services provided for the purposes of the NHS by any other NHS foundation trust that provides services under this Act to the commissioner,",

(c) in paragraph 15(4), after the new subsection (2C) to be inserted into that section, insert—

"(2D) Where the administrator recommends taking action in relation to another NHS foundation trust, the references in subsection (2A) to a commissioner also include a reference to a person to which the other NHS foundation trust provides services under this Act that would be affected by the action.

(2E) A service provided by an NHS foundation trust is an essential service for the purposes of subsection (2A) if the person making the statement in question is satisfied that the criterion in section 65DA(3) is met.

(2F) Section 65DA(4) applies to the person making the statement when that person is determining whether that criterion is met.",

(d) in paragraph 15, after sub-paragraph (7) insert—

"(8) Omit subsections (8) to (10).",

(e) in paragraph 16 (the text of which becomes sub-paragraph (1)) at the end insert—

"(2) In subsection (4)(a)(ii) of that section, omit "or NHS trust".

(3) In subsection (7) of that section, omit "or an NHS trust" and "or the NHS trust".

(4) In subsection (8) of that section, omit "or an NHS trust".",

(f) in paragraph 17, in sub-paragraph (2)(a), for "paragraph (b)" substitute "paragraphs (b), (bzb), (bzc) and (bzd)",

(g) in that paragraph, after sub-paragraph (4) insert—

"(4A) In subsection (11A)—

(a) omit paragraph (a), and

(b) in paragraph (b), omit "where the trust in question is an NHS foundation trust," and ", or an NHS trust,".",

(h) in paragraph 24, after sub-paragraph (2) insert—

"(2A) Omit subsection (1A).",

(i) after that paragraph insert—

"24A In section 65O (interpretation)—

(a) omit subsection (2), and

(b) in subsection (3), omit "or an NHS trust".", and

(j) in paragraph 35, omit the "and" preceding paragraph (d) and after that paragraph insert ", and

(e) in subsection (6), omit "makes a decision under section 65K(1),"."

PART 4

HEALTH AND SOCIAL CARE

Integration fund

121 Integration of care and support with health services etc: integration fund

(1) At the end of section 223B of the National Health Service Act 2006 (funding of the National Health Service Commissioning Board) insert—

"(6) Where the mandate specifies objectives relating to service integration, the requirements that may be specified under section 13A(2)(b) include such requirements relating to the use by the Board of an amount of the sums paid to it under this section as the Secretary of State considers it necessary or expedient to impose.

(7) The amount referred to in subsection (6)—

(a) is to be determined in such manner as the Secretary of State considers appropriate, and

(b) must be specified in the mandate.

(8) The reference in subsection (6) to service integration is a reference to the integration of the provision of health services with the provision of health-related services or social care services, as referred to in sections 13N and 14Z1."

(2) After section 223G of that Act (meeting expenditure of clinical commissioning groups out of public funds) insert—

"223GA Expenditure on integration

(1) Where the mandate includes a requirement in reliance on section 223B(6) (requirements relating to use by the Board of an amount paid to the Board

where mandate specifies service integration objectives), the Board may direct a clinical commissioning group that an amount (a "designated amount") of the sums paid to the group under section 223G is to be used for purposes relating to service integration.

(2) The designated amount is to be determined—

(a) where the mandate includes a requirement (in reliance on section 223B(6)) that designated amounts are to be determined by the Board in a manner specified in the mandate, in that manner;

(b) in any other case, in such manner as the Board considers appropriate.

(3) The conditions under section 223G(7) subject to which the payment of a designated amount is made must include a condition that the group transfers the amount into one or more funds ("pooled funds") established under arrangements under section 75(2)(a) ("pooling arrangements").

(4) The conditions may also include—

(a) conditions relating to the preparation and agreement by the group and each local authority and other clinical commissioning group that is party to the pooling arrangements of a plan for how to use the designated amount (a "spending plan");

(b) conditions relating to the approval of a spending plan by the Board;

(c) conditions relating to the inclusion of performance objectives in a spending plan;

(d) conditions relating to the meeting of any performance objectives included in a spending plan or specified by the Board.

(5) Where a condition subject to which the payment of a designated amount is made is not met, the Board may—

(a) withhold the payment (in so far as it has not been made);

(b) recover the payment (in so far as it has been made);

(c) direct the clinical commissioning group as to the use of the designated amount for purposes relating to service integration or for making payments under section 256.

(6) Where the Board withholds or recovers a payment under subsection (5)(a) or (b)—

(a) it may use the amount for purposes consistent with such objectives and requirements relating to service integration as are specified in the mandate, and

(b) in so far as the exercise of the power under paragraph (a) involves making a payment to a different clinical commissioning group or some other person, the making of the payment is subject to such conditions as the Board may determine.

(7) The requirements that may be specified in the mandate in reliance on section 223B(6) include requirements to consult the Secretary of State or other specified persons before exercising a power under subsection (5) or (6).

(8) The power under subsection (5)(b) to recover a payment may be exercised in a financial year after the one in respect of which the payment was made.

(9) The payments that may be made out of a pooled fund into which a designated amount is transferred include payments to a local authority which is not party

to the pooling arrangements in question in connection with the exercise of its functions under Part 1 of the Housing Grants, Construction and Regeneration Act 1996 (disabilities facilities grants).

(10) In exercising a power under this section, the Board must have regard to the extent to which there is a need for the provision of each of the following—

(a) health services (see subsection (12)),

(b) health-related services (within the meaning given in section 14Z1), and

(c) social care services (within the meaning given in that section).

(11) A reference in this section to service integration is a reference to the integration of the provision of health services with the provision of health-related services or social care services, as referred to in sections 13N and 14Z1.

(12) "Health services" means services provided as part of the health service in England.".

Information

122 The Health and Social Care Information Centre: restrictions on dissemination of information

(1) Chapter 2 of Part 9 of the Health and Social Care Act 2012 (the Health and Social Care Information Centre) is amended as follows.

(2) In section 253(1) (general duties), after paragraph (c) (but before the "and" after it) insert—

"(ca) the need to respect and promote the privacy of recipients of health services and of adult social care in England,".

(3) In section 261 (other dissemination of information), after subsection (1) insert—

"(1A) But the Information Centre may do so only if it considers that disseminating the information would be for the purposes of—

(a) the provision of health care or adult social care, or

(b) the promotion of health."

(4) After section 262 insert—

"262A Publication and other dissemination: supplementary

In exercising any function under this Act of publishing or otherwise disseminating information, the Information Centre must have regard to any advice given to it by the committee appointed by the Health Research Authority under paragraph 8(1) of Schedule 7 to the Care Act 2014 (committee to advise in connection with information dissemination etc)."

PART 5

GENERAL

123 Power to make consequential provision

(1) The Secretary of State may by order make provision in consequence of a provision of this Act.

(2) An order under this section may amend, repeal, or revoke an enactment, or provide for an enactment to apply with specified modifications.

(3) The power conferred by this section is not restricted by any other provision of this Act.

(4) A saving or a transitional or transitory provision in an order under this section by virtue of section 125(8) may, in particular, modify the application of a provision made by the order pending the commencement of—

- (a) another provision of the order,
- (b) a provision of this Act, or
- (c) any other enactment.

(5) Before making an order under this section that contains provision which is within the legislative competence of a devolved legislature, the Secretary of State must consult the relevant devolved authority.

(6) A reference to an enactment includes a reference to an enactment passed or made after the passing of this Act.

124 Power to make transitional etc. provision

(1) The Secretary of State may by order make transitional, transitory or saving provision in connection with the commencement of a provision of this Act.

(2) An order under this section may modify the application of a provision of this Act pending the commencement of—

- (a) another provision of this Act, or
- (b) any other enactment (including one passed or made after the passing of this Act).

125 Regulations and orders

(1) A power to make regulations under this Act is exercisable by the Secretary of State.

(2) Regulations and orders under this Act must be made by statutory instrument.

(3) Subject to subsections (4) and (6), a statutory instrument containing regulations or an order under this Act is subject to annulment in pursuance of a resolution of either House of Parliament.

(4) A statutory instrument which contains (whether alone or with other provision) any of the following may not be made unless a draft of the instrument has been laid before, and approved by a resolution of, each House of Parliament—

- (a) regulations under section 13(7) (the eligibility criteria);

(b) regulations under section 15(4) (the cap on care costs) other than those made in discharge of the duty under section 16(1);

(c) the first regulations under section 15(8) (the amount attributable to an adult's daily living costs);

(d) regulations under section 22(2)(b) (services or facilities which a local authority may not provide or arrange);

(e) regulations under section 35(9) or 36(3) (deferred payment agreements and loans and alternative financial arrangements) which include provision that amends or repeals a provision of an Act of Parliament, or provides for a provision of an Act of Parliament to apply with modifications;

(f) the first regulations under section 52(12) (meaning of references to business failure);

(g) the first regulations under section 53(1) (criteria for application of market oversight regime);

(h) the first regulations under section 53(4) (disapplication of market oversight regime in particular cases);

(i) the first regulations under section 62(2) (exercise of power to meet child's carer's needs for support);

(j) the first regulations under section 72 (Part 1 appeals);

(k) subsequent regulations under that section which include provision that amends or repeals a provision of an Act of Parliament, or provides for a provision of an Act of Parliament to apply with modifications;

(l) an order under section 79(9) (delegation of local authority functions);

(m) regulations under section 92 (offence of supplying etc false or misleading information);

(n) an order under section 123 (consequential provision) which includes provision that amends or repeals a provision of an Act of Parliament, or provides for a provision of an Act of Parliament to apply with modifications;

(o) regulations under paragraph 18 of Schedule 7 (fees chargeable by the HRA).

(5) Subsection (4) does not apply to a statutory instrument which contains regulations or an order within paragraph (e), (k) or (n) of that subsection, if the regulations or order are within the paragraph in question only because they include provision that applies an Act of Parliament with modifications for the purpose of making saving, transitional or transitory provision.

(6) Subsection (3) does not apply to—

(a) an order under section 96 (transfer order to new HEE);

(b) an order under section 109 (transfer order to new HRA);

(c) an order under section 124 (transitional etc. provision);

(d) an order under section 127 (commencement).

(7) A power to make regulations or an order under this Act—

(a) may be exercised for all cases to which the power applies, for those cases subject to specified exceptions, or for any specified cases or descriptions of case,

(b) may be exercised so as to make, for the cases for which it is exercised—

(i) the full provision to which the power applies or any less provision (whether by way of exception or otherwise);

(ii) the same provision for all cases for which the power is exercised, or different provision for different cases or different descriptions of case, or different provision as respects the same case or description of case for different purposes of this Act;

(iii) any such provision either unconditionally or subject to specified conditions, and

(c) may, in particular, make different provision for different areas.

(8) A power to make regulations or an order under this Act (other than the power to make an order under section 124 or 127) includes —

(a) power to make incidental, supplementary, consequential, saving, transitional or transitory provision, and

(b) power to provide for a person to exercise a discretion in dealing with a matter.

(9) Before making regulations under section 52(12) (meaning of references to business failure), the Secretary of State must consult the Welsh Ministers and the Department for Health, Social Services and Public Safety in Northern Ireland.

126 General interpretation

In this Act—

"devolved authority" means the Scottish Ministers, the Welsh Ministers or the Department for Health, Social Services and Public Safety in Northern Ireland,

"devolved legislature" means the Scottish Parliament, the National Assembly for Wales or the Northern Ireland Assembly,

"enactment" includes—

(a) an enactment contained in subordinate legislation (within the meaning of the Interpretation Act 1978), and

(b) an enactment contained in, or in an instrument made under, an Act of the Scottish Parliament, an Act or Measure of the National Assembly for Wales or Northern Ireland legislation,

"financial year" means a period of 12 months ending with 31 March (but see also the definition of that expression in paragraph 3 of Schedule 2, paragraph 19 of Schedule 5 and paragraph 19 of Schedule 7), and

"the health service" means the comprehensive health service in England continued under section 1(1) of the National Health Service Act 2006.

127 Commencement

(1) The provisions of Parts 1 to 4 come into force on such day as the Secretary of State may by order appoint.

(2) The provisions of this Part come into force on the day on which this Act is passed.

(3) Before making an order under this section bringing section 50 (provider failure: temporary duty on local authority in Wales in cross-border cases) or 75 (after-care under the Mental Health Act 1983) into force, the Secretary of State must obtain the consent of the Welsh Ministers.

(4) Before making an order under this section bringing section 51 (provider failure: temporary duty on Health and Social Care trusts in cross-border cases) into force,

the Secretary of State must obtain the consent of the Department for Health, Social Services and Public Safety in Northern Ireland.

(5) Different days may be appointed under subsection (1) for different purposes (including different areas).

128 Extent and application

(1) This Act extends to England and Wales only, subject to subsections (2) and (3).

(2) Any amendment, repeal or revocation made by this Act has the same extent as the enactment being amended, repealed or revoked, other than the amendment made by section 66(3) which extends to England and Wales only.

(3) The following also extend to Scotland and Northern Ireland—

(a) section 39(8) and Schedule 1 (cross-border placements);

(b) sections 49 to 52 (provider failure: temporary duty in relation to cross-border cases);

(c) section 73 (Human Rights Act 1998: provision of regulated care or support etc a public function);

(d) Chapter 2 of Part 3 (the HRA);

(e) section 118 (transfer orders), so far as relating to section 109 (the HRA);

(f) section 119 (Chapters 1 and 2 of Part 3: interpretation and supplementary provision);

(g) this Part;

(h) paragraph 17 of Schedule 5 (arrangements between HEE and devolved authorities) and section 96(2) so far as relating to that paragraph.

(4) The Secretary of State may by order provide that specified provisions of this Act, in their application to the Isles of Scilly, have effect with such modifications as may be specified.

129 Short title

This Act may be cited as the Care Act 2014.

SCHEDULES

SCHEDULE 1

Section 39

CROSS-BORDER PLACEMENTS

Placements from England to Wales, Scotland or Northern Ireland

1 (1) Where a local authority in England is meeting an adult's needs for care and support by arranging for the provision of accommodation in Wales, the adult—

(a) is to be treated for the purposes of this Part as ordinarily resident in the local authority's area, and

(b) is accordingly not to be treated for the purposes of the Social Services and Well-being (Wales) Act 2014 as ordinarily resident anywhere in Wales.

(2) Where a local authority in England, in reliance on section 22(4), is making arrangements which include the provision of accommodation in Wales, section 22(4) is to have effect as if for paragraph (a) there were substituted—

"(a) the authority has obtained consent for it to arrange for the provision of the nursing care from the Local Health Board for the area in which the accommodation is provided,".

(3) Where a local authority in England is meeting an adult's needs for care and support by arranging for the provision of accommodation in Scotland—

(a) the adult is to be treated for the purposes of this Part as ordinarily resident in the local authority's area, and

(b) no duty under Part 2 of the Social Work (Scotland) Act 1968 or sections 25 to 27 of the Mental Health (Care and Treatment) (Scotland) Act 2003 applies in the adult's case.

(4) Where a local authority in England is meeting an adult's needs for care and support by arranging for the provision of accommodation in Northern Ireland—

(a) the adult is to be treated for the purposes of this Part as ordinarily resident in the local authority's area, and

(b) no duty under the Health and Personal Social Services (Northern Ireland) Order 1972 or the Health and Social Care (Reform) Act (Northern Ireland) 2009 to provide or secure the provision of accommodation or other facilities applies in the adult's case.

(5) Section 22 (prohibition on provision of health services) is to have effect—

(a) in its application to a case within sub-paragraph (1)—

(i) as if the references in subsections (1) and (6) to the National Health Service Act 2006 included a reference to the National Health Service (Wales) Act 2006, and

(ii) as if the reference in subsection (6) to a clinical commissioning group or the National Health Service Commissioning Board included a reference to a Local Health Board;

(b) in its application to a case within sub-paragraph (3)—

(i) as if the references in subsections (1) and (6) to the National Health Service Act 2006 included a reference to the National Health Service (Scotland) Act 1978, and

(ii) as if the reference in subsection (6) to a clinical commissioning group or the National Health Service Commissioning Board included a reference to a Health Board or Special Health Board;

(c) in its application to a case within sub-paragraph (4)—

(i) as if the references in subsections (1) and (6) to a service or facility provided under the National Health Service Act 2006 included a reference to health care provided under the Health and Personal Social Services (Northern Ireland) Order 1972 or the Health and Social Care (Reform) Act (Northern Ireland) 2009, and

(ii) as if the reference in subsection (6) to a clinical commissioning group or the National Health Service Commissioning Board included a reference to a Health and Social Care trust.

(6) Regulations may make further provision in relation to arrangements of the kind referred to in this paragraph.

(7) The regulations may specify circumstances in which, in a case within sub-paragraph (3), specified duties under Part 2 of the Social Work (Scotland) Act 1968 are nonetheless to apply in the case of the adult concerned (and paragraph (b) of that sub-paragraph is to be read accordingly).

Placements from Wales to England, Scotland or Northern Ireland

2 (1) Where a local authority in Wales is discharging its duty under section 35 of the Social Services and Well-being (Wales) Act 2014 by arranging for the provision of accommodation in England, the adult concerned—

(a) is to be treated for the purposes of that Act as ordinarily resident in the local authority's area, and

(b) is accordingly not to be treated for the purposes of this Part of this Act as ordinarily resident anywhere in England.

(2) Where a local authority in Wales is arranging for the provision of accommodation in England in the exercise of its power under section 36 of the Social Services and Well-being (Wales) Act 2014—

(a) the adult concerned is to be treated for the purposes of that Act—

(i) in a case where the adult was within the local authority's area immediately before being provided by the local authority with accommodation in England, as remaining within that area;

(ii) in a case where the adult was outside but ordinarily resident in the local authority's area immediately before being provided by the local authority with accommodation in England, as remaining outside but ordinarily resident in that area, and

(b) the adult concerned is not to be treated for the purposes of this Part of this Act as ordinarily resident anywhere in England (unless the adult was so ordinarily resident immediately before being provided by the local authority with accommodation in England).

(3) Where a local authority in Wales is discharging its duty under section 35 of the Social Services and Well-being (Wales) Act 2014 by arranging for the provision of accommodation in Scotland—

(a) the adult is to be treated for the purposes of that Act as ordinarily resident in the local authority's area, and

(b) no duty under Part 2 of the Social Work (Scotland) Act 1968 or sections 25 to 27 of the Mental Health (Care and Treatment) (Scotland) Act 2003 applies in the adult's case.

(4) Where a local authority in Wales is arranging for the provision of accommodation in Scotland in the exercise of its power under section 36 of the Social Services and Well-being (Wales) Act 2014—

(a) the adult concerned is to be treated for the purposes of that Act—

(i) in a case where the adult was within the local authority's area immediately before being provided by the local authority with accommodation in Scotland, as remaining within that area;

(ii) in a case where the adult was outside but ordinarily resident in the local authority's area immediately before being provided by the local authority with accommodation in Scotland, as remaining outside but ordinarily resident in that area, and

(b) no duty under Part 2 of the Social Work (Scotland) Act 1968 or sections 25 to 27 of the Mental Health (Care and Treatment) (Scotland) Act 2003 applies in the adult's case.

(5) But paragraph (b) of sub-paragraph (4) does not prevent a duty mentioned in that paragraph from applying in the case of an adult who was ordinarily resident in Scotland immediately before being provided by the local authority with accommodation in Scotland.

(6) Where a local authority in Wales is discharging its duty under section 35 of the Social Services and Well-being (Wales) Act 2014 by arranging for the provision of accommodation in Northern Ireland—

(a) the adult is to be treated for the purposes of that Act as ordinarily resident in the local authority's area, and

(b) no duty under the Health and Personal Social Services (Northern Ireland) Order 1972 or the Health and Social Care (Reform) Act (Northern Ireland) 2009 to provide or secure the provision of accommodation or other facilities applies in the adult's case.

(7) Where a local authority in Wales is arranging for the provision of accommodation in Northern Ireland in the exercise of its power under section 36 of the Social Services and Well-being (Wales) Act 2014—

(a) the adult concerned is to be treated for the purposes of that Act—

(i) in a case where the adult was within the local authority's area immediately before being provided by the local authority with accommodation in Northern Ireland, as remaining within that area;

(ii) in a case where the adult was outside but ordinarily resident in the local authority's area immediately before being provided by the local authority with accommodation in Northern Ireland, as remaining outside but ordinarily resident in that area, and

(b) no duty under the Health and Personal Social Services (Northern Ireland) Order 1972 or the Health and Social Care (Reform) Act (Northern Ireland) 2009 to provide or secure the provision of accommodation or other facilities applies in the adult's case.

(8) But paragraph (b) of sub-paragraph (7) does not prevent a duty mentioned in that paragraph from applying in the case of an adult who was ordinarily resident in Northern Ireland immediately before being provided by the local authority with accommodation in Northern Ireland.

(9) Regulations may make further provision in relation to arrangements of the kind referred to in this paragraph.

(10) The regulations may specify circumstances in which, in a case within sub-paragraph (3) or (4), specified duties under Part 2 of the Social Work (Scotland) Act 1968 are nonetheless to apply in the case of the adult concerned (and paragraph (b) of each of those sub-paragraphs is to be read accordingly).

Placements from Scotland to England, Wales or Northern Ireland

3 (1) Where a local authority in Scotland is discharging its duty under section 12 or 13A of the Social Work (Scotland) Act 1968 or section 25 of the Mental Health (Care and Treatment) (Scotland) Act 2003 by securing the provision of accommodation in England, the adult in question is not to be treated for the purposes of this Part of this Act as ordinarily resident anywhere in England.

(2) Where a local authority in Scotland is discharging its duty under a provision referred to in sub-paragraph (1) by securing the provision of accommodation in Wales, the adult in question is not to be treated for the purposes of the Social Services and Well-being (Wales) Act 2014 as ordinarily resident anywhere in Wales.

(3) Where a local authority in Scotland is discharging its duty under a provision referred to in sub-paragraph (1) by securing the provision of accommodation in Northern Ireland, no duty under the Health and Personal Social Services (Northern Ireland) Order 1972 or the Health and Social Care (Reform) Act (Northern Ireland) 2009 to provide or secure the provision of accommodation or other facilities applies in the case of the adult in question.

(4) In section 5 of the Community Care and Health (Scotland) Act 2002 (local authority arrangements for residential accommodation outside Scotland)—

(a) in subsection (1), after "the 1968 Act" insert "or under section 25 of the Mental Health (Care and Treatment) (Scotland) Act 2003 (care and support)",

(b) in subsection (2), for "such arrangements" substitute "persons for whom such arrangements are made", and

(c) for subsections (5) and (6) substitute—

> "(5) In subsections (1) and (3) above, "appropriate establishment" means an establishment of such description or conforming to such requirements as may be specified in regulations under subsection (1)."

(5) Regulations may make further provision in relation to arrangements of the kind referred to in this paragraph.

Placements from Northern Ireland to England, Wales or Scotland

4 (1) Where there are arrangements under Article 15 of the Health and Personal Social Services (Northern Ireland) Order 1972 for the provision of accommodation in England, the adult in question—

(a) is to be treated for the purposes of that Order and the Health and Social Care (Reform) Act (Northern Ireland) 2009 as ordinarily resident in the area of the relevant Health and Social Care trust, and

(b) is accordingly not to be treated for the purposes of this Part of this Act as ordinarily resident anywhere in England.

(2) Where there are arrangements under Article 15 of the Health and Personal Social Services (Northern Ireland) Order 1972 for the provision of accommodation in Wales, the adult in question—

(a) is to be treated for the purposes of that Order and the Health and Social Care (Reform) Act (Northern Ireland) 2009 as ordinarily resident in the area of the relevant Health and Social Care trust, and

(b) is accordingly not to be treated for the purposes of the Social Services and Well-being (Wales) Act 2014 as ordinarily resident anywhere in Wales.

(3) Where there are arrangements under Article 15 of the Health and Personal Social Services (Northern Ireland) Order 1972 for the provision of accommodation in Scotland—

(a) the adult in question is to be treated for the purposes of that Order and the Health and Social Care (Reform) Act (Northern Ireland) 2009 as ordinarily resident in the area of the relevant Health and Social Care trust, and

(b) no duty under Part 2 of the Social Work (Scotland) Act 1968 or sections 25 to 27 of the Mental Health (Care and Treatment) (Scotland) Act 2003 applies in the adult's case.

(4) The reference to the relevant Health and Social Care trust is a reference to the Health and Social Care trust in whose area the adult in question was ordinarily resident immediately before the making of arrangements of the kind referred to in this paragraph.

(5) Regulations may make further provision in relation to arrangements of the kind referred to in this paragraph.

(6) The regulations may specify circumstances in which, in a case within sub-paragraph (3), specified duties under Part 2 of the Social Work (Scotland) Act 1968 are nonetheless to apply in the case of the adult concerned (and paragraph (b) of that sub-paragraph is to be read accordingly).

Dispute resolution

5 (1) Any dispute about the application of any of paragraphs 1 to 4 to an adult's case is to be determined in accordance with this paragraph.

(2) If the dispute is between a local authority in England and a local authority in Wales, it is to be determined by the Secretary of State or the Welsh Ministers.

(3) If the dispute is between a local authority in England and a local authority in Scotland, it is to be determined by the Secretary of State or the Scottish Ministers.

(4) If the dispute is between a local authority in England and a Health and Social Care trust, it is to be determined by the Secretary of State or the Northern Ireland Department.

(5) If the dispute is between a local authority in Wales and a local authority in Scotland, it is to be determined by the Welsh Ministers or the Scottish Ministers.

(6) If the dispute is between a local authority in Wales and a Health and Social Care trust, it is to be determined by the Welsh Ministers or the Northern Ireland Department.

(7) If the dispute is between a local authority in Scotland and a Health and Social Care trust, it is to be determined by the Scottish Ministers or the Northern Ireland Department.

(8) In Article 36 of the Health and Personal Social Services (Northern Ireland) Order 1972, after paragraph (2) insert—

> "(2A) Any question under this Order as to the ordinary residence of a person is to be determined by the Department."

(9) Regulations must make provision for determining which of the persons concerned is to determine the dispute; and the regulations may, in particular, provide for the dispute to be determined by whichever of them they agree is to do so.

(10) Regulations may make provision for the determination of disputes between more than two parties.

(11) Regulations may make further provision about determination of disputes under this paragraph or under regulations under sub-paragraph (10); the regulations may, for example, include—

(a) provision requiring parties to a dispute to take specified steps before referring the dispute for determination under this paragraph;

(b) provision about the procedure for referring the dispute under this paragraph.

Financial adjustments

6 (1) This paragraph applies where—

(a) an adult has been provided with accommodation in England, Wales, Scotland or Northern Ireland, and

(b) it transpires (whether following the determination of a dispute under paragraph 5 or otherwise) that an authority in another of the territories was, for some or all of the time that the accommodation was being provided, liable to provide the adult with accommodation.

(2) The authority which made the arrangements may recover from the authority in the other territory the amount of any payments it made towards the making of the arrangements at a time when the other authority was liable to provide the adult with accommodation.

(3) A reference to an authority is a reference to a local authority in England, Wales or Scotland or a Health and Social Care trust in Northern Ireland.

7 (1) In section 86 of the Social Work (Scotland) Act 1968 (adjustments between authorities providing accommodation), in subsections (1) and (10), after "a local

authority in England or Wales" insert "and to a Health and Social Care trust in Northern Ireland".

(2) In subsection (2) of that section, after "the ordinary residence of a person shall" insert ", in a case where there is a dispute about the application of any of paragraphs 1 to 4 of Schedule 1 to the Care Act 2014 (cross-border placements), be determined in accordance with paragraph 5 of that Schedule; and in any other case, the question shall".

(3) After subsection (10) of that section insert—

"(10A) A person who, as a result of Schedule 1 to the Care Act 2014 (cross-border placements), is treated as ordinarily resident in an area in England, Wales or Northern Ireland (as the case may be) is to be treated as ordinarily resident in that area for the purposes of this section.

(10B) A person who, as a result of that Schedule, is not treated as ordinarily resident anywhere in England or Wales (as the case may be) is not to be treated as ordinarily resident there for the purposes of this section."

(4) In section 97 of that Act (extent)—

(a) in subsection (1), for "sections 86 and 87" substitute "section 87", and

(b) after that subsection insert—

"(1A) Section 86 of this Act shall extend to England and Wales and to Northern Ireland."

Provision of NHS accommodation not to affect deemed ordinary residence etc.

8 (1) In a case where, as a result of this Schedule, an adult is treated as ordinarily resident in an area in England, Wales or Northern Ireland (as the case may be), the adult does not cease to be so treated merely because the adult is provided with NHS accommodation.

(2) In a case where, as a result of this Schedule, an adult is not treated as ordinarily resident anywhere in England or Wales (as the case may be), the adult continues not to be so treated even if the adult is provided with NHS accommodation.

(3) In a case where, as a result of this Schedule, no duty under a relevant enactment applies, the duty does not apply merely because the adult in question is provided with NHS accommodation; and for this purpose "relevant enactment" means—

(a) Part 2 of the Social Work (Scotland) Act 1968,

(b) sections 25 to 27 of the Mental Health (Care and Treatment) (Scotland) Act 2003,

(c) the Health and Personal Social Services (Northern Ireland) Order 1972, or

(d) the Health and Social Care (Reform) Act (Northern Ireland) 2009.

(4) In a case where, as a result of paragraph 2(2), (4) or (7), an adult is treated as remaining within, or as remaining outside but ordinarily resident in, an area in Wales, the adult does not cease to be so treated merely because the adult is provided with NHS accommodation.

Direct payments

9 (1) Regulations may provide for this Schedule to apply, with such modifications as may be specified, to a case where accommodation in England, Wales, Scotland or Northern Ireland is provided for an adult by means of direct payments made by an authority in another of the territories.

(2) The reference in sub-paragraph (1) to direct payments accordingly includes a reference to direct payments made—

(a) under section 50 or 52 of the Social Services and Well-being (Wales) Act 2014,

(b) as a result of a choice made by the adult pursuant to section 5 of the Social Care (Self-directed Support) (Scotland) Act 2013, or

(c) by virtue of section 8 of the Carers and Direct Payments Act (Northern Ireland) 2002.

Particular types of accommodation

10 (1) Regulations may provide for this Schedule to apply, with such modifications as may be specified, to a case where—

(a) an adult has needs for care and support which can be met only if the adult is living in accommodation of a type specified in the regulations,

(b) the adult is living in accommodation in England, Wales, Scotland or Northern Ireland that is of a type so specified, and

(c) the adult's needs for care and support are being met by an authority in another of the territories providing or arranging for the provision of services other than the accommodation.

(2) In section 5 of the Community Care and Health (Scotland) Act 2002 (the title to which becomes "Local authority arrangements for residential accommodation etc. outwith Scotland"), in subsection (1), at the end insert "or for the provision in England and Wales or in Northern Ireland of a service or facility of such other description as may be specified in the regulations".

Regulations

11 Regulations under this Schedule—

(a) if they include provision relating to Wales, may not be made without the consent of the Welsh Ministers;

(b) if they include provision relating to Scotland, may not be made without the consent of the Scottish Ministers;

(c) if they include provision relating to Northern Ireland, may not be made without the consent of the Northern Ireland Department.

Interpretation

12 (1) This paragraph applies for the purposes of this Schedule.

(2) "Accommodation in England" means accommodation in England of a type specified in regulations under section 39 but not of a type specified in regulations under this paragraph.

(3) "Accommodation in Wales" means accommodation in Wales of a type specified in regulations under section 194 of the Social Services and Well-being (Wales) Act 2014 but not of a type specified in regulations under this paragraph.

(4) "Accommodation in Scotland" means residential accommodation in Scotland of a type which may be provided under or by virtue of section 12 or 13A of the Social Work (Scotland) Act 1968, or section 25 of the Mental Health (Care and Treatment) (Scotland) Act 2003, but not of a type specified in regulations under this paragraph.

(5) "Accommodation in Northern Ireland" means residential or other accommodation in Northern Ireland of a type which may be provided under Article 15 of the Health and Personal Social Services (Northern Ireland) Order 1972.

(6) "Local authority in England" means a local authority for the purposes of this Part.

(7) "Local authority in Wales" means a local authority for the purposes of the Social Services and Well-being (Wales) Act 2014.

(8) "Local authority in Scotland" means a council constituted under section 2 of the Local Government etc. (Scotland) Act 1994.

(9) "The Northern Ireland Department" means the Department of Health, Social Services and Public Safety in Northern Ireland.

(10) "NHS accommodation" has the meaning given in section 39(6).

Consequential provision

13 In section 194 of the Social Services and Well-being (Wales) Act 2014 (ordinary residence), at the end insert—

"(8) For provision about cross-border placements to and from England, Scotland or Northern Ireland, see Schedule 1 to the Care Act 2014.

(8) Am ddarpariaeth ynghylch lleoliadau trawsffiniol i Loegr, yr Alban neu Ogledd Iwerddon neu o Loegr, yr Alban neu Ogledd Iwerddon, gweler Atodlen 1 i Ddeddf Gofal 2014."

Transitory provision

14 (1) Pending the commencement of Part 4 of the Social Services and Well-being (Wales) Act 2014, this Schedule is to have effect with the modifications set out in this paragraph.

(2) A reference to that Act in paragraphs 1, 3 and 4 is to be read as a reference to Part 3 of the National Assistance Act 1948.

(3) In paragraph 2—

(a) the references in sub-paragraphs (1), (3) and (6) to discharging a duty under section 35 of the Social Services and Well-being (Wales) Act 2014 by arranging for the provision of accommodation are to be read as references to providing residential accommodation under Part 3 of the National Assistance Act 1948;

(b) the references in paragraph (a) of each of those sub-paragraphs to the Social Services and Well-being (Wales) Act 2014 are to be read as references to Part 3 of the National Assistance Act 1948;

(c) sub-paragraphs (2), (4) and (7) are to be ignored; and

(d) in sub-paragraph (10), the references to sub-paragraph (4) and paragraph (b) of sub-paragraph (4) are to be ignored.

(4) In paragraph 9, the reference to sections 50 and 52 of the Social Services and Well-being (Wales) Act 2014 is to be read as a reference to section 57 of the Health and Social Care Act 2001.

(5) In paragraph 12, sub-paragraph (3) is to be read as if the following were substituted for it—

"(3) Accommodation in Wales" means residential accommodation in Wales of a type that may be provided under Part 3 of the National Assistance Act 1948 but not of a type specified in regulations under this paragraph."

(6) In that paragraph, sub-paragraph (7) is to be read as if the following were substituted for it—

"(7) Local authority in Wales" means a local authority in Wales for the purposes of Part 3 of the National Assistance Act 1948."

(7) This paragraph does not affect the generality of section 124(2).

SCHEDULE 2

Section 43

SAFEGUARDING ADULTS BOARDS

Membership, etc.

1 (1) The members of an SAB are—

(a) the local authority which established it,

(b) a clinical commissioning group the whole or part of whose area is in the local authority's area,

(c) the chief officer of police for a police area the whole or part of which is in the local authority's area, and

(d) such persons, or persons of such description, as may be specified in regulations.

(2) The membership of an SAB may also include such other persons as the local authority which established it, having consulted the other members listed in sub-paragraph (1), considers appropriate.

(3) A local authority, having consulted the other members of its SAB, must appoint as the chair a person whom the authority considers to have the required skills and experience.

(4) Each member of an SAB must appoint a person to represent it on the SAB; and the representative must be a person whom the member considers to have the required skills and experience.

(5) Where more than one clinical commissioning group or more than one chief officer of police comes within sub-paragraph (1), a person may represent more than one of the clinical commissioning groups or chief officers of police.

(6) The members of an SAB (other than the local authority which established it) must, in acting as such, have regard to such guidance as the Secretary of State may issue.

(7) Guidance for the local authority on acting as a member of the SAB is to be included in the guidance issued for the purposes of section 78(1).

(8) An SAB may regulate its own procedure.

Funding and other resources

2 (1) A member of an SAB listed in paragraph 1(1) may make payments towards expenditure incurred by, or for purposes connected with, the SAB—

(a) by making the payments directly, or

(b) by contributing to a fund out of which the payments may be made.

(2) A member of an SAB listed in paragraph 1(1) may provide staff, goods, services, accommodation or other resources for purposes connected with the SAB.

Strategic plan

3 (1) An SAB must publish for each financial year a plan (its "strategic plan") which sets out—

(a) its strategy for achieving its objective (see section 43), and

(b) what each member is to do to implement that strategy.

(2) In preparing its strategic plan, the SAB must—

(a) consult the Local Healthwatch organisation for its area, and

(b) involve the community in its area.

(3) In this paragraph and paragraph 4, "financial year", in relation to an SAB, includes the period—

(a) beginning with the day on which the SAB is established, and

(b) ending with the following 31 March or, if the period ending with that date is 3 months or less, ending with the 31 March following that date.

Annual report

4 (1) As soon as is feasible after the end of each financial year, an SAB must publish a report on—

(a) what it has done during that year to achieve its objective,

(b) what it has done during that year to implement its strategy,

(c) what each member has done during that year to implement the strategy,

(d) the findings of the reviews arranged by it under section 44 (safeguarding adults reviews) which have concluded in that year (whether or not they began in that year),

(e) the reviews arranged by it under that section which are ongoing at the end of that year (whether or not they began in that year),

(f) what it has done during that year to implement the findings of reviews arranged by it under that section, and

(g) where it decides during that year not to implement a finding of a review arranged by it under that section, the reasons for its decision.

(2) The SAB must send a copy of the report to—

(a) the chief executive and the leader of the local authority which established the SAB,

(b) the local policing body the whole or part of whose area is in the local authority's area,

(c) the Local Healthwatch organisation for the local authority's area, and

(d) the chair of the Health and Wellbeing Board for that area.

(3) "Local policing body" has the meaning given by section 101 of the Police Act 1996.

SCHEDULE 3

Section 74

Discharge of hospital patients with care and support needs

Cases where hospital patient is likely to have care and support needs after discharge

1 (1) Where the NHS body responsible for a hospital patient considers that it is not likely to be safe to discharge the patient unless arrangements for meeting the patient's needs for care and support are in place, the body must give notice to—

(a) the local authority in whose area the patient is ordinarily resident, or

(b) if it appears to the body that the patient is of no settled residence, the local authority in whose area the hospital is situated.

(2) A notice under sub-paragraph (1) is referred to in this Schedule as an "assessment notice"; and the local authority to which an assessment notice is given is referred to in this Schedule as "the relevant authority".

(3) An assessment notice—

(a) must describe itself as such, and

(b) may not be given more than seven days before the day on which the patient is expected to be admitted to hospital.

(4) Before giving an assessment notice, the NHS body responsible for the patient must consult—

(a) the patient, and

(b) where it is feasible to do so, any carer that the patient has.

(5) An assessment notice remains in force until—

(a) the patient is discharged (whether by the NHS body responsible for the patient or by the patient himself or herself),

(b) the patient dies, or

(c) the NHS body responsible for the patient withdraws the notice by giving a notice (a "withdrawal notice") to the relevant authority.

(6) A reference in this paragraph to a hospital patient includes a reference to a person who it is reasonable to expect is about to become one.

Assessment notice given by responsible NHS body to local authority

2 (1) The NHS body responsible for a hospital patient, having given the relevant authority an assessment notice, must—

(a) consult the authority before deciding what it will do for the patient in order for discharge to be safe, and

(b) give the authority notice of the day on which it proposes to discharge the patient.

(2) A notice under sub-paragraph (1)(b) is referred to in this Schedule as a "discharge notice".

(3) A discharge notice must specify—

(a) whether the NHS body responsible for the patient will be providing or arranging for the provision of services under the National Health Service Act 2006 to the patient after discharge, and

(b) if it will, what those services are.

(4) A discharge notice remains in force until—

(a) the end of the relevant day, or

(b) the NHS body responsible for the patient withdraws the notice by giving a withdrawal notice to the relevant authority.

(5) The "relevant day" is the later of—

(a) the day specified in the discharge notice, and

(b) the last day of such period as regulations may specify.

(6) A period specified under sub-paragraph (5)(b) must—

(a) begin with the day after that on which the assessment notice is given, and

(b) last for a period of at least two days.

3 (1) The relevant authority, having received an assessment notice and having in light of it carried out a needs assessment and (where applicable) a carer's assessment, must inform the NHS body responsible for the patient—

(a) whether the patient has needs for care and support,

(b) (where applicable) whether a carer has needs for support,

(c) whether any of the needs referred to in paragraphs (a) and (b) meet the eligibility criteria, and

(d) how the authority plans to meet such of those needs as meet the eligibility criteria.

(2) Where, having carried out a needs assessment or carer's assessment in a case within section 27(4), the relevant authority considers that the patient's needs for care and support or (as the case may be) the carer's needs for support have changed, it must inform the NHS body responsible for the patient of the change.

Cases where discharge of the patient is delayed

4 (1) If the relevant authority, having received an assessment notice and a discharge notice, has not carried out a needs or (where applicable) carer's assessment and the patient has not been discharged by the end of the relevant day, the NHS body responsible for the patient may require the relevant authority to pay the specified amount for each day of the specified period.

(2) If the relevant authority has not put in place arrangements for meeting some or all of those of the needs under sections 18 to 20 that it proposes to meet in the case of the patient or (where applicable) a carer, and the patient has for that reason alone not been discharged by the end of the relevant day, the NHS body responsible for the patient may require the relevant authority to pay the specified amount for each day of the specified period.

(3) If, in a case within sub-paragraph (1) or (2), the assessment notice ceases to be in force, any liability arising under that sub-paragraph before it ceased to be in force is unaffected.

(4) A payment under sub-paragraph (1) or (2) must be made to—

(a) the NHS body responsible for the patient, or

(b) in such a case as regulations may specify, the person specified.

(5) The "relevant day" has the meaning given by paragraph 2(5).

(6) A reference to a requirement to pay the specified amount is a reference to a requirement to pay the amount specified in regulations; and the reference to the specified period is a reference to the period specified in or determined in accordance with regulations.

(7) In specifying the amount of a payment, the Secretary of State must have regard in particular to either or both of—

(a) costs to NHS bodies of providing accommodation and personal care to patients ready to be discharged, and

(b) costs to local authorities of meeting needs under sections 18 to 20 in the case of persons who have been discharged.

Delegation to management of independent hospital

5 (1) An NHS body may make arrangements with any person connected with the management of an independent hospital for that person (or an employee of that person) to do, on behalf of the NHS body and in accordance with the arrangements, anything which is required or authorised to be done by the NHS body by or under this Schedule in relation to hospital patients accommodated in that hospital.

(2) Anything done or omitted to be done by or in relation to the authorised person (or an employee of that person) under such arrangements is to be treated as done or omitted to be done by or in relation to the NHS body.

(3) Nothing in this paragraph prevents anything being done by or in relation to the NHS body.

Adjustments between local authorities

6 (1) Regulations may modify, or otherwise make provision about, the application of a provision of this Schedule in a case where it appears to the NHS body responsible for a hospital patient that the patient is ordinarily resident in the area of another local authority.

(2) The regulations may, in particular, authorise or require a local authority—

(a) to accept an assessment notice given to it even though it may wish to dispute that it was the correct authority to which to give the notice;

(b) to become the relevant authority in the patient's case;

(c) to recover expenditure incurred—

(i) in the exercise of functions under this Schedule;

(ii) in meeting needs under sections 18 to 20 in a case under this Schedule.

Meaning of "hospital patient", "NHS hospital, "NHS body", etc.

7 (1) A hospital patient is a person ordinarily resident in England who—

(a) is being accommodated at an NHS hospital, or at an independent hospital as a result of arrangements made by an NHS body, and

(b) is receiving (or has received or can reasonably be expected to receive) acute care.

(2) "NHS hospital" means a health service hospital (as defined by the National Health Service Act 2006) in England.

(3) "Independent hospital" means a hospital (as defined by that Act) in the United Kingdom which is not—

(a) an NHS hospital,

(b) a health service hospital as defined by section 206 of the National Health Service (Wales) Act 2006,

(c) a health service hospital as defined by section 108 of the National Health Service (Scotland) Act 1978, or

(d) a hospital vested in the Department of Health, Social Services and Public Safety in Northern Ireland or managed by a Health and Social Care trust.

(4) "NHS body" means—

(a) an NHS trust established under section 25 of the National Health Service Act 2006,

(b) an NHS foundation trust,

(c) the National Health Service Commissioning Board, or

(d) a clinical commissioning group.

(5) A reference to the NHS body responsible for a hospital patient is—

(a) if the hospital is an NHS hospital, a reference to the NHS body managing it, or

(b) if the hospital is an independent hospital, a reference to the NHS body that arranged for the patient to be accommodated in it.

(6) "Acute care" means intensive medical treatment provided by or under the supervision of a consultant, that lasts for a limited period after which the person receiving the treatment no longer benefits from it.

(7) Care is not "acute care" if the patient has given an undertaking (or one has been given on the patient's behalf) to pay for it; nor is any of the following "acute care"—

(a) care of an expectant or nursing mother;

(b) mental health care;

(c) palliative care;

(d) a structured programme of care provided for a limited period to help a person maintain or regain the ability to live at home;

(e) care provided for recuperation or rehabilitation.

(8) "Mental health care" means psychiatric services, or other services provided for the purpose of preventing, diagnosing or treating illness, the arrangements for which are the primary responsibility of a consultant psychiatrist.

Further provision about assessment notices, discharge notices, etc.

8 Regulations may—

(a) specify the form and content of an assessment notice, a discharge notice or a withdrawal notice;

(b) specify the manner in which an assessment notice, a discharge notice or a withdrawal notice may be given;

(c) specify when a discharge notice may be given;

(d) specify circumstances in which a withdrawal notice must be given;

(e) make provision for determining the day on which an assessment notice, a discharge notice or a withdrawal notice is to be regarded as given.

SCHEDULE 4

Section 75

DIRECT PAYMENTS: AFTER-CARE UNDER THE MENTAL HEALTH ACT 1983

PART 1

AFTER-CARE UNDER THE MENTAL HEALTH ACT 1983: DIRECT PAYMENTS

1 (1) Sections 31 (adults with capacity to request direct payments), 32 (adults without capacity to request direct payments) and 33 (direct payments: further provision) apply in relation to section 117 of the Mental Health Act 1983 but as if the following modifications were made to those sections.

(2) For subsection (1) of section 31, substitute—

"(1) This section applies where an adult to whom section 117 of the Mental Health Act 1983 (after-care) applies requests the local authority to make payments to the adult or a person nominated by the adult that are equivalent to the cost of providing or arranging for the provision of after-care services for the adult under that section."

(3) In subsection (5) of that section—

(a) in paragraph (a), for "meeting the adult's needs" substitute "discharging its duty under section 117 of the Mental Health Act 1983", and

(b) in paragraph (b), for "to meet the adult's needs" substitute "to discharge its duty under that section".

(4) In subsection (7) of that section, for "to meet the needs in question" substitute "to discharge its duty under section 117 of the Mental Health Act 1983".

(5) For subsection (1) of section 32, substitute—

"(1) This section applies where—

(a) an adult to whom section 117 of the Mental Health Act 1983 (after-care) applies lacks capacity to request the local authority to make payments equivalent to the cost of providing or arranging for the provision of after-care services for the adult under that section, and

(b) an authorised person requests the local authority to make such payments to the authorised person."

(6) In subsection (4)(a) of that section, for "the adult's needs for care and support" substitute "the provision to the adult of after-care services under section 117 of the Mental Health Act 1983".

(7) In subsection (6) of that section—

(a) in paragraph (a), for "meeting the adult's needs" substitute "discharging its duty under section 117 of the Mental Health Act 1983", and

(b) in paragraph (b), for "to meet the adult's needs" substitute "to discharge its duty under that section".

(8) In subsection (7) of that section, for "the provision of the care and support" substitute "the provision of after-care services under section 117 of the Mental Health Act 1983".

(9) In subsection (9) of that section, for "to meet the needs in question" substitute "to discharge its duty under section 117 of the Mental Health Act 1983".

(10) In subsection (2)(a) of section 33, for "meet needs" substitute "discharge its duty under section 117 of the Mental Health Act 1983".

(11) For subsection (3) of that section, substitute—

"(3) A direct payment is made on condition that it be used only to pay for arrangements under which after-care services for the adult are provided under section 117 of the Mental Health Act 1983."

PART 2

Provision to be inserted in Social Services and Well-being (Wales) Act 2014

"SCHEDULE A1

Direct payments: after-care under the Mental Health Act 1983

1 General

1 Sections 50 (direct payments to meet an adult's needs), 51 (direct payments to meet a child's needs) and 53 (direct payments: further provision) apply in relation to section 117 of the Mental Health Act 1983 but as if the following modifications were made to those sections.

2 Modifications to section 50

2 For subsection (1) of section 50 substitute—

"(1) Regulations may require or allow a local authority to make payments to an adult to whom section 117 of the Mental Health Act 1983 (after-care) applies that are equivalent to the cost of providing or arranging for the provision of after-care services for the adult under that section."

3 In subsection (3) of that section—

(a) in paragraph (a), for "who has needs for care and support ("A")" substitute "in respect of the provision to the adult ("A") of after-care services under section 117 of the Mental Health Act 1983", and

(b) in paragraph (c)(i), for "of meeting A's needs" substitute "of discharging its duty towards A under section 117 of the Mental Health Act 1983".

4 In subsection (4) of that section—

(a) in paragraph (a), for "who has needs for care and support ("A")" substitute "to whom section 117 of the Mental Health Act 1983 applies ("A")", and

(b) in paragraph (d)(i), for "meeting A's needs" substitute "discharging its duty towards A under section 117 of the Mental Health Act 1983".

5 In subsection (5) of that section—

(a) in paragraph (a), for "A's needs for care and support" substitute "the provision to A of after-care services under section 117 of the Mental Health Act 1983", and

(b) in paragraph (b), for "towards the cost of meeting A's needs for care and support" substitute "equivalent to the cost of providing or arranging the provision to A of after-care services under section 117 of the Mental Health Act 1983".

6 In subsection (6)(b) of that section, for "A's needs for care and support" substitute "the provision to A of after-care services under section 117 of the Mental Health Act 1983".

7 Modifications to section 51

7 For subsection (1) of section 51 substitute—

"(1) Regulations may require or allow a local authority to make payments to a person in respect of a child to whom section 117 of the Mental Health Act 1983 (after-care) applies that are equivalent to the cost of providing or arranging the provision of after-care services for the child under that section."

8 In subsection (3)(a) and (b) of that section, for "who has needs for care and support" (in each place it occurs) substitute "to whom section 117 of the Mental Health Act 1983 applies".

9 In subsection (5)(a) of that section, for "meeting the child's needs" substitute "discharging its duty towards the child under section 117 of the Mental Health Act 1983".

10 Modifications to section 53

10 In subsection (1) of section 53—

(a) in the opening words, for "50, 51 or 52" substitute "50 or 51",

(b) omit paragraphs (a), (b) and (c),

(c) in paragraph (i), for "a local authority's duty or power to meet a person's needs for care and support or a carer's needs for support is displaced" substitute "a local authority's duty under section 117 of the Mental Health Act 1983 (after-care) is discharged", and

(d) in paragraph (k), for "50 to 52" substitute "50 and 51".

11 Omit subsections (2) to (8) of that section.

12 After subsection (8) of that section insert—

"(8A) Regulations under sections 50 and 51 must specify that direct payments to meet the cost of providing or arranging for the provision of after-care services under section 117 of the Mental Health Act 1983 (after-care) must be made at a rate that the local authority estimates to be equivalent to the reasonable cost of securing the provision of those services to meet those needs."

13 In subsection (9) of that section—

(a) for ", 51 or 52" substitute "or 51", and

(b) for "care and support (or, in the case of a carer, support)" substitute "after-care services".

14 In subsection (10) of that section, for "care and support (or, in the case of a carer, support) to meet needs" substitute "after-care services"."

SCHEDULE 5

Section 96

HEALTH EDUCATION ENGLAND

PART 1

CONSTITUTION

Membership

1 (1) HEE consists of—

(a) a chair appointed by the Secretary of State,

(b) six other members appointed by the Secretary of State,

(c) a chief executive appointed by the members appointed under paragraphs (a) and (b), and

(d) no more than four other members appointed by the members appointed under paragraphs (a) and (b).

(2) The members appointed under sub-paragraph (1)(a) and (b)—

(a) are not employees of HEE, and

(b) are referred to in this Schedule as the "non-executive members".

(3) The members appointed under sub-paragraph (1)(c) and (d)—

(a) are employees of HEE, and

(b) are referred to in this Schedule as the "executive members".

2 (1) The members of HEE must include persons who have clinical expertise of a description specified in regulations.

(2) The regulations may require—

(a) a specified number of members to have that expertise;

(b) a specified number of non-executive members to have that expertise;
(c) a specified number of executive members to have that expertise.

(3) The non-executive members of HEE must include a person who will represent the interests of patients.

Non-executive members: terms of office

3 (1) A person holds office as a non-executive member of HEE on the terms of that person's appointment.

(2) A person may not be appointed as a non-executive member for a period of more than four years.

(3) A person who ceases to be a non-executive member is eligible for re-appointment.

(4) A person may resign from office as a non-executive member by giving notice to the Secretary of State.

(5) The Secretary of State may remove a person from office as a non-executive member on any of the following grounds—
(a) incapacity;
(b) misbehaviour;
(c) failure to carry out his or her duties as a non-executive member.

(6) The Secretary of State may suspend a person from office as a non-executive member if it appears to the Secretary of State that there are or may be grounds to remove that person from office under sub-paragraph (5).

Non-executive members: suspension from office

4 (1) Having decided to suspend a person under paragraph 3(6), the Secretary of State must give notice of the decision to the person; and the suspension takes effect when the person receives the notice.

(2) The notice may be—
(a) delivered in person (in which case the person is taken to receive it when it is delivered), or
(b) sent by first class post to the person's last known address (in which case, the person is taken to receive it on the third day after the day on which it is posted).

(3) The initial period of suspension must not exceed six months.

(4) The Secretary of State may review the suspension.

(5) The Secretary of State—
(a) must review the suspension, if requested in writing by the person to do so, but
(b) need not review the suspension less than three months after the beginning of the initial period of suspension.

(6) Following a review during a period of suspension, the Secretary of State may—
(a) revoke the suspension, or
(b) suspend the person for a period of no more than six months from the expiry of the current period.

(7) The Secretary of State must revoke the suspension if the Secretary of State—

(a) decides that there are no grounds to remove the person from office under paragraph 3(5), or

(b) decides that there are grounds to do so but nonetheless decides not to do so.

5 (1) Where a person is suspended from office as the chair under paragraph 3(6), the Secretary of State may appoint a non-executive member as interim chair to exercise the chair's functions.

(2) Appointment as interim chair is for a term not exceeding the shorter of—

(a) the period ending with either—

(i) the appointment of a new chair, or

(ii) the revocation or expiry of the existing chair's suspension, and

(b) the remainder of the interim chair's term as a non-executive member.

(3) A person who ceases to be the interim chair is eligible for re-appointment.

Non-executive members: pay

6 (1) HEE must pay its non-executive members such remuneration as the Secretary of State may decide.

(2) HEE must pay, or provide for the payment of, such allowances or gratuities as the Secretary of State may decide to a person who is or has been a non-executive member of HEE.

Employees: terms of office

7 (1) Each executive member of HEE is appointed as an employee of HEE on such terms as it decides.

(2) A person may not be appointed as chief executive without the consent of the Secretary of State.

(3) HEE may appoint, on such terms as it decides, other persons as employees of HEE (in addition to those appointed as executive members).

Employees: pay

8 (1) HEE must pay its employees such remuneration as it decides.

(2) HEE may pay, or provide for the payment of, such pensions, allowances or gratuities as it decides to or in respect of a person who is or has been an employee of HEE.

(3) Before making a decision about pay under this paragraph, HEE must obtain the approval of the Secretary of State to its policy on the matter.

Committees and sub-committees

9 (1) HEE may appoint committees and sub-committees.

(2) A committee or sub-committee may consist of or include persons who are not members or employees of HEE.

(3) HEE may pay such remuneration and allowances as it decides to a person who is a member of a committee (including a committee which HEE is required to appoint under section 103(1) (LETBs)) or sub-committee, but is not an employee of HEE, regardless of whether the person is a non-executive member of HEE.

(4) Any committees and sub-committees of the Special Health Authority called Health Education England in existence immediately before its abolition are to become respectively committees and sub-committees of HEE (and are to be treated as appointed under this paragraph).

Procedure

10 (1) HEE may regulate its own procedure.

(2) A vacancy among the members of HEE, or a defect in the appointment of a member, does not affect the validity of any act of HEE.

Seal and evidence

11 (1) The application of HEE's seal must be authenticated by the signature of a member of HEE or a person who has been authorised (whether generally or specifically) for the purpose.

(2) A document purporting to be duly executed under HEE's seal or to be signed on its behalf must be received in evidence and, unless the contrary is proved, taken to be so executed or signed.

(3) But this paragraph does not apply in relation to a document which is, or is to be, signed in accordance with the law of Scotland.

Status of HEE

12 (1) HEE is not to be regarded as a servant or agent of the Crown, or as enjoying any status, privilege or immunity of the Crown.

(2) HEE's property is not to be regarded as property of, or property held on behalf of, the Crown.

PART 2

FUNCTIONS

Exercise of functions

13 (1) HEE must exercise its functions effectively, efficiently and economically.

(2) HEE may arrange for any of its committees, sub-committees or members or any other person to exercise any of its functions on its behalf (but see sub-paragraph (5)).

(3) HEE may arrange for any person to help it to exercise its functions (whether in a particular case or in cases of a particular description).

(4) Arrangements under sub-paragraph (2) or (3) may provide for the payment of remuneration and allowances to the persons with whom HEE makes the arrangements.

(5) HEE may not arrange for a committee which is not an LETB, or for a sub-committee, member or any other person, to exercise a function which is exercisable by an LETB.

(6) HEE may in any way it thinks appropriate involve health care workers, persons to whom health services are provided or carers for such persons, in decisions it makes about the exercise of its functions; and "carer" means an adult who provides or intends to provide care for another person.

(7) HEE may do anything which appears to it to be necessary or desirable for the purposes of or in connection with the exercise of its functions.

(8) In section 247C of the National Health Service Act 2006 (Secretary of State's duty to keep health service functions of certain bodies under review), in subsection (2), after paragraph (e) insert—

"(ea) Health Education England;".

Help or advice for other public authorities

14 (1) HEE may provide help or advice to another public authority for the purpose of the exercise by that authority of its functions.

(2) Help or advice under this paragraph may be provided on such terms as HEE decides (including terms relating to payment of remuneration or allowances).

(3) "Public authority"—

(a) includes any person certain of whose functions are functions of a public nature, but

(b) does not include either House of Parliament or a person exercising functions in connection with proceedings in Parliament.

(4) A reference to a public authority—

(a) includes a public authority in the Channel Islands or the Isle of Man, but

(b) subject to that, does not include a reference to a public authority outside the United Kingdom.

Co-operation

15 (1) HEE must, in the exercise of its functions, co-operate with the Secretary of State in the exercise of the Secretary of State's public health functions (as defined by section 1H of the National Health Service Act 2006).

(2) In section 72 of that Act (co-operation between NHS bodies), after subsection (3) insert—

"(4) For the purposes of this section, Health Education England is an NHS body."

(3) In section 290(3) of the Health and Social Care Act 2012 (bodies which must co-operate with Monitor and the Care Quality Commission in the exercise of their functions), after paragraph (c) (but before the following "and") insert—

"(ca) Health Education England,".

(4) Regulations may require HEE and a specified person to co-operate with each other in the exercise of their respective functions or such of their functions as are specified.

NHS contracts

16 In section 9(4) of the National Health Service Act 2006 (NHS contracts: health service bodies), after paragraph (kb) insert—

"(kc) Health Education England,".

Arrangements with devolved authorities

17 (1) HEE may arrange with a devolved authority for HEE—

(a) to exercise on behalf of the devolved authority any function which corresponds to a function of HEE;

(b) to provide services or facilities in so far as the devolved authority requires them in connection with the exercise of such a function.

(2) The terms and conditions on which arrangements under this paragraph may be made include provision for payment to HEE in respect of its costs in giving effect to the arrangements.

Failure to exercise functions

18 (1) If the Secretary of State considers that HEE is failing or has failed to exercise any of its functions, and that the failure is significant, the Secretary of State may direct HEE to exercise such of its functions, in such manner and within such period, as the direction specifies.

(2) If HEE fails to comply with a direction under this section, the Secretary of State may—

(a) exercise the functions specified in the direction, or

(b) make arrangements for some other person to exercise them on the Secretary of State's behalf.

(3) Where the Secretary of State exercises a power under sub-paragraph (1) or (2), the Secretary of State must publish the reasons for doing so.

(4) The reference in sub-paragraph (1) to exercising a function includes a reference to exercising it properly.

PART 3

FINANCE AND REPORTS

Funding

19 (1) The Secretary of State must pay HEE for each financial year sums not exceeding the amount the Secretary of State has allotted for that year towards meeting the expenditure that is attributable to HEE's exercise of its functions in that year.

(2) An amount is to be regarded as allotted when the Secretary of State notifies HEE accordingly.

(3) The Secretary of State may make a new allotment under this paragraph increasing or decreasing the allotment previously made, but only if—

(a) HEE agrees,

(b) a parliamentary general election takes place, or

(c) the Secretary of State considers that exceptional circumstances make a new allotment necessary.

(4) The Secretary of State may give directions to HEE about the payment by it to the Secretary of State of sums in respect of charges or other amounts relating to the valuation or disposal of assets.

(5) Sums payable to HEE under this paragraph are payable subject to such conditions as to records, certificates or otherwise as the Secretary of State may decide.

(6) In this Part of this Schedule, "financial year" includes the period—

(a) beginning with the day on which HEE is established, and

(b) ending with the following 31 March or, if the period ending with that date is 3 months or less, ending with the 31 March following that date.

Financial duties: expenditure

20 (1) HEE must ensure that total expenditure attributable to its exercise of its functions in each financial year (its "total spending") does not exceed the aggregate of—

(a) the amount allotted to it for that year under paragraph 19,

(b) the income generated in that year from carrying out activities for the purposes of or in connection with the exercise of its functions, and

(c) any other sums received by it in that year for the purpose of enabling it to meet such expenditure.

(2) The Secretary of State may direct that spending of a specified description is, or is not, to be treated for the purposes of sub-paragraph (1) as part of HEE's total spending.

(3) The Secretary of State may by directions determine—

(a) the extent to which, and circumstances in which, sums received by HEE under paragraph 19 but not yet spent are to be treated for the purposes of sub-paragraph (1) as part of HEE's total spending, and

(b) to which financial year those sums are to be attributed.

(4) The Secretary of State may direct HEE to use specified banking facilities for specified purposes.

Financial duties: use of generated income

21 Where HEE generates income from carrying out activities for the purposes of or in connection with the exercise of its functions, it must ensure that the income is used for exercising its functions.

Financial duties: controls on total resource use

22 (1) HEE must ensure that—

(a) its use of capital resources in a financial year does not exceed the amount specified by the Secretary of State, and

(b) its use of revenue resources in a financial year does not exceed the amount specified by the Secretary of State.

(2) The Secretary of State may, in relation to a financial year, direct that for the purposes of this paragraph—

(a) resources of a specified description are, or are not, to be treated as capital resources or revenue resources;

(b) a specified use of capital resources or revenue resources is, or is not, to be taken into account.

(3) An amount specified for the purposes of sub-paragraph (1)(a) or (b) may be varied only if—

(a) HEE agrees,

(b) a parliamentary general election takes place, or

(c) the Secretary of State considers that exceptional circumstances make the variation necessary.

(4) A reference to the use of capital resources or revenue resources is a reference to their expenditure, consumption or reduction in value.

Financial duties: additional controls on resource use

23 (1) The Secretary of State may direct HEE to ensure that—

(a) total capital resource use in a financial year which is attributable to specified matters does not exceed a specified amount,

(b) total revenue resource use in a financial year which is attributable to specified matters does not exceed a specified amount, and

(c) total revenue resource use in a financial year which is attributable to specified matters relating to administration does not exceed a specified amount.

(2) The Secretary of State may give directions, in relation to a financial year, specifying uses of capital resources or revenue resources which are, or are not, to be taken into account for the purposes of sub-paragraph (1)(a), (b) or (c) (as the case may be).

(3) The Secretary of State may not give a direction under sub-paragraph (1)(a) or (b) unless the direction is for the purpose of complying with a limit imposed by the Treasury.

Losses and liabilities etc

24 (1) Section 265 of the Public Health Act 1875 (which relates to the protection of members and officers of certain authorities from personal liability) has effect as if there were included in the authorities referred to in that section a reference to HEE.

(2) In its application to HEE as a result of sub-paragraph (1), section 265 of that Act has effect as if any reference in that section to that Act were a reference to this Act.

(3) In section 71(2) of the National Health Service Act 2006 (schemes for meeting losses and liabilities etc of certain health service bodies: bodies eligible to participate), after paragraph (db) insert—

"(dc) Health Education England,".

Accounts

25 (1) HEE must keep—

(a) proper accounts, and

(b) proper records relating to the accounts.

(2) The Secretary of State may, with the approval of the Treasury, give directions to HEE about—

(a) the content and form of its accounts, and

(b) the methods and principles to be applied in the preparation of its accounts.

(3) The reference in sub-paragraph (2) to accounts includes a reference to—

(a) the accounts prepared under paragraph 26, and

(b) such accounts as are prepared under paragraph 27.

(4) The chief executive of HEE is to be its accounting officer.

Annual accounts

26 (1) HEE must prepare consolidated annual accounts for each financial year.

(2) The consolidated annual accounts must include—

(a) the annual accounts of each LETB,

(b) the annual accounts of each other committee of HEE, and

(c) the annual accounts relating to the rest of HEE's activities.

(3) HEE must send copies of the consolidated annual accounts to—

(a) the Secretary of State, and

(b) the Comptroller and Auditor General,

within such period after the end of the financial year to which the accounts relate as the Secretary of State directs.

(4) The Comptroller and Auditor General must—

(a) examine, certify and report on the consolidated annual accounts, and

(b) lay copies of them and the report on them before Parliament.

Interim accounts

27 (1) The Secretary of State may, with the approval of the Treasury, direct HEE to prepare accounts in respect of such period or periods as are specified in the direction ("interim accounts").

(2) The interim accounts in respect of any period must include—

(a) the accounts of each LETB in respect of that period, and

(b) the accounts of each other committee of HEE in respect of that period.

(3) HEE must send copies of any interim accounts to—

(a) the Secretary of State, and

(b) if the Secretary of State directs, the Comptroller and Auditor General,

within such period as the Secretary of State may direct.

(4) The Comptroller and Auditor General must—

(a) examine, certify and report on any interim accounts sent under sub-paragraph (3)(b),

(b) if the Secretary of State directs, send a copy of the report on the accounts to the Secretary of State, and

(c) if the Secretary of State directs, lay copies of the accounts and the report on them before Parliament.

Annual report

28 (1) As soon as is feasible after the end of each financial year, HEE must prepare an annual report on how it has exercised its functions during the year.

(2) The report must include, in particular, HEE's assessment of—

(a) the extent to which is has during the year—

(i) achieved the objectives and reflected the priorities set by the Secretary of State for the purposes of section 100(1); and

(ii) achieved the outcomes set by the Secretary of State for the purposes of section 100(2); and

(b) how effectively it discharged its duties under this Act or under regulations under this Act.

(3) HEE must—

(a) lay a copy of the report before Parliament, and

(b) send a copy of it to the Secretary of State.

(4) HEE must provide the Secretary of State with such other reports and information relating to the exercise of its functions as the Secretary of State may request.

PART 4

CONSEQUENTIAL AMENDMENTS

Public Records Act 1958

29 In Part 2 of the Table in Schedule 1 to the Public Records Act 1958, at the appropriate place insert—

"Health Education England."

Public Bodies (Admission to Meetings) Act 1960

30 In the Schedule to the Public Bodies (Admission to Meetings) Act 1960, after paragraph (bl) insert—

"(bm) Health Education England;".

Parliamentary Commissioner Act 1967

31 In Schedule 2 to the Parliamentary Commissioner Act 1967, at the appropriate place insert—

"Health Education England".

House of Commons Disqualification Act 1975

32 In Part 2 of Schedule 1 to the House of Commons Disqualification Act 1975, at the appropriate place insert—

"Health Education England."

Copyright, Designs and Patents Act 1988

33 In section 48(6) of the Copyright, Designs and Patents Act 1988 (definition of "the Crown"), after "the Care Quality Commission" insert ", Health Education England".

Freedom of Information Act 2000

34 In Part 3 of Schedule 1 to the Freedom of Information Act 2000 (health service), at the appropriate place insert—

"Health Education England."

Equality Act 2010

35 In Part 1 of Schedule 19 to the Equality Act 2010 (authorities subject to the public sector equality duty), in the group of entries under the heading "Health, social care and social security", before the entry for the Health Service Commissioner for England, insert—

"Health Education England."

SCHEDULE 6

Section 104

LOCAL EDUCATION AND TRAINING BOARDS

The area for which an LETB is appointed

1 (1) HEE must ensure that the areas of LETBs—

(a) do not coincide or overlap, and

(b) together cover the whole of England.

(2) HEE may vary the area of an LETB.

(3) HEE must—

(a) keep an up-to-date record of the area of each LETB, and

(b) publish the record.

Assessment of whether the appointment criteria are being met in relation to LETBs

2 (1) HEE must, whenever it considers appropriate, assess—

(a) whether the appointment criteria are being met in relation to an LETB, and

(b) if they are not, whether enough of the appointment criteria are being met for the LETB in question to be able to exercise its functions.

(2) Having carried out an assessment under sub-paragraph (1), HEE must notify the LETB of, and then publish—

(a) the result of the assessment, and

(b) if HEE is not satisfied that the criteria are being met in relation to the LETB, HEE's reasons for not being so satisfied.

(3) Where, on an assessment under sub-paragraph (1), HEE is not satisfied that all the appointment criteria are being met in relation to an LETB but is satisfied that enough of them are being met for the LETB to be able to exercise its functions, HEE may impose conditions on the LETB relating to its operation.

(4) Where, on an assessment under sub-paragraph (1), HEE is not satisfied that enough of the appointment criteria are being met in relation to the LETB for the LETB to be able to exercise its functions, HEE may do one or more of the following—

(a) appoint new members of the LETB (whether as well as or instead of existing members);

(b) exercise functions on behalf of the LETB;

(c) make arrangements for the persons who provide health services in the area for which the LETB was appointed to be represented by another LETB instead.

(5) Before imposing conditions under sub-paragraph (3) or taking action under sub-paragraph (4), HEE must notify the LETB concerned of—

(a) the conditions it proposes to impose or action it proposes to take, and

(b) its reasons for proposing to impose those conditions or take that action.

(6) Having imposed conditions under sub-paragraph (3) or taken action under sub-paragraph (4), HEE must publish—

(a) details of the conditions it imposed or action it took, and

(b) its reasons for imposing those conditions or taking that action.

(7) Before making arrangements under sub-paragraph (4)(c), HEE must obtain the approval of the other LETB.

(8) Regulations must require specified commissioners of health services to include in the arrangements under the National Health Service Act 2006 for the provision of such services terms to ensure that a provider of such services—

(a) co-operates with any LETB which represents that provider by virtue of arrangements made by HEE under sub-paragraph (4)(c), in such manner and to such extent as that LETB may request, in planning the provision of, and in providing, education and training for health care workers;

(b) provides that LETB with such information as it may request.

(9) Regulations may specify other circumstances in which HEE may intervene in the operation of an LETB (whether by imposing conditions or in such other way as is specified).

(10) A reference to exercising a function includes a reference to exercising it properly.

Publication and review of the appointment criteria

3 (1) HEE must publish the appointment criteria; but before doing so it must obtain the approval of the Secretary of State.

(2) HEE must keep the appointment criteria under review and may revise them; and the duty to obtain approval under sub-paragraph (1) applies to revised criteria only in so far as HEE considers the revisions significant.

Exercise of functions

4 (1) Regulations may—

(a) give LETBs additional functions relating to the provision of education and training for health care workers or to the planning of its provision;

(b) impose requirements on LETBs relating to how they exercise functions.

(2) An LETB may do anything which appears to it to be necessary or desirable for the purposes of or in connection with the exercise of its functions.

(3) If HEE considers that an LETB is failing or has failed to exercise a function, or that there is a significant risk that it will fail to do so, HEE must direct the LETB to exercise such function within such period, and in such manner, as the direction specifies.

(4) If an LETB fails to comply with a direction under sub-paragraph (3), HEE may take action under one or more of paragraphs (a) to (c) of paragraph 2(4) (with paragraph 2(5) to (7) applying accordingly).

(5) The reference in sub-paragraph (3) to exercising a function includes a reference to exercising it properly.

SCHEDULE 7

Section 109

THE HEALTH RESEARCH AUTHORITY

PART 1

CONSTITUTION

Membership

1 (1) The HRA consists of—

(a) a chair appointed by the Secretary of State,

(b) at least three but no more than four other members appointed by the Secretary of State,

(c) a chief executive appointed by the members appointed under paragraphs (a) and (b), and

(d) at least two but no more than three other members appointed by the members appointed under paragraphs (a) and (b).

(2) The members appointed under sub-paragraph (1)(a) and (b)—

(a) are not employees of the HRA, and

(b) are referred to in this Schedule as the "non-executive members".

(3) The members appointed under sub-paragraph (1)(c) and (d)—

(a) are employees of the HRA, and

(b) are referred to in this Schedule as the "executive members".

(4) The number of non-executive members must exceed the number of executive members.

Non-executive members: terms of office

2 (1) A person holds office as a non-executive member of the HRA on the terms of that person's appointment.

(2) A person may not be appointed as a non-executive member for a period of more than four years.

(3) A person who ceases to be a non-executive member is eligible for re-appointment.

(4) A person may resign from office as a non-executive member by giving notice to the Secretary of State.

(5) The Secretary of State may remove a person from office as a non-executive member on any of the following grounds—

(a) incapacity;

(b) misbehaviour;

(c) failure to carry out his or her duties as a non-executive member.

(6) The Secretary of State may suspend a person from office as a non-executive member if it appears to the Secretary of State that there are or may be grounds to remove that person from office under sub-paragraph (5).

Non-executive members: suspension from office

3 (1) Having decided to suspend a person under paragraph 2(6), the Secretary of State must give notice of the decision to the person; and the suspension takes effect when the person receives the notice.

(2) The notice may be—

(a) delivered in person (in which case the person is taken to receive it when it is delivered), or

(b) sent by first class post to the person's last known address (in which case, the person is taken to receive it on the third day after the day on which it is posted).

(3) The initial period of suspension must not exceed six months.

(4) The Secretary of State may review the suspension.

(5) The Secretary of State—

(a) must review the suspension, if requested in writing by the person to do so, but

(b) need not review the suspension less than three months after the beginning of the initial period of suspension.

(6) Following a review during a period of suspension, the Secretary of State may—

(a) revoke the suspension, or

(b) suspend the person for a period of no more than six months from the expiry of the current period.

(7) The Secretary of State must revoke the suspension if the Secretary of State—

(a) decides that there are no grounds to remove the person from office under paragraph 2(5), or

(b) decides that there are grounds to do so but nonetheless decides not to do so.

4 (1) Where a person is suspended from office as the chair under paragraph 2(6), the Secretary of State may appoint a non-executive member as interim chair to exercise the chair's functions.

(2) Appointment as interim chair is for a term not exceeding the shorter of—

(a) the period ending with either—

(i) the appointment of a new chair, or

(ii) the revocation or expiry of the existing chair's suspension, and

(b) the remainder of the interim chair's term as a non-executive member.

(3) A person who ceases to be the interim chair is eligible for re-appointment.

Non-executive members: pay

5 (1) The HRA must pay its non-executive members such remuneration as the Secretary of State may decide.

(2) The HRA must pay, or provide for the payment of, such allowances or gratuities as the Secretary of State may decide to a person who is or has been a non-executive member of the HRA.

Employees: terms of office

6 (1) Each executive member of the HRA is appointed as an employee of the HRA on such terms as it decides.

(2) A person may not be appointed as chief executive without the consent of the Secretary of State.

(3) The HRA may appoint, on such terms as it decides, other persons as employees of the HRA (in addition to those appointed as executive members).

Employees: pay

7 (1) The HRA must pay its employees such remuneration as it decides.

(2) The HRA may pay, or provide for the payment of, such pensions, allowances or gratuities as it decides to or in respect of a person who is or has been an employee of the HRA.

(3) Before making a decision about pay under this paragraph, the HRA must obtain the approval of the Secretary of State to its policy on the matter.

Committees and sub-committees

8 (1) The HRA must appoint a committee for the purpose of giving advice—

(a) to the HRA in connection with the exercise of the HRA's function under regulation 5(1)(a) of the Health Service (Control of Patient Information) Regulations 2002 (S.I. 2002/1438) (approval for processing confidential patient information);

(b) to the Secretary of State in connection with the exercise of the Secretary of State's functions under regulations 2, 3(4) and 5 of those Regulations (processing of confidential patient information);

(c) to the Health and Social Care Information Centre in connection with—

(i) the exercise by the Centre of functions conferred in regulations under section 251 of the National Health Service Act 2006 (processing of patient information for medical purposes);

(ii) any publication or other dissemination by the Centre of information which is in a form which identifies an individual to whom the information relates or enables the identity of such an individual to be ascertained.

(2) The HRA may appoint other committees and sub-committees.

(3) The committee appointed under sub-paragraph (1) must consist of persons who are not members or employees of the HRA.

(4) Any other committee or sub-committee may consist of or include such persons.

(5) The HRA may pay such remuneration and allowances as it decides to a person who is a member of a committee or sub-committee, but is not an employee of the HRA, regardless of whether the person is a non-executive member of the HRA.

9 Regulations may provide for the committee appointed under paragraph 8(1) to be required, in giving advice, to have regard to specified factors or matters.

Procedure

10 (1) The HRA may regulate its own procedure.

(2) A vacancy among the members of the HRA, or a defect in the appointment of a member, does not affect the validity of any act of the HRA.

Seal and evidence

11 (1) The application of the HRA's seal must be authenticated by the signature of a member of the HRA or a person who has been authorised (whether generally or specifically) for the purpose.

(2) A document purporting to be duly executed under the HRA's seal or to be signed on its behalf must be received in evidence and, unless the contrary is proved, taken to be so executed or signed.

(3) But this paragraph does not apply in relation to a document which is, or is to be, signed in accordance with the law of Scotland.

Status of the HRA

12 (1) The HRA is not to be regarded as a servant or agent of the Crown, or as enjoying any status, privilege or immunity of the Crown.

(2) The HRA's property is not to be regarded as property of, or property held on behalf of, the Crown.

PART 2

FUNCTIONS

Exercise of functions

13 (1) The HRA must exercise its functions effectively, efficiently and economically.

(2) The HRA may arrange for any of its committees, sub-committees or members or any other person (other than a devolved authority) to exercise any of its functions on its behalf.

(3) The HRA may arrange for any person to help it in the exercise of its functions (whether in a particular case or in cases of a particular description).

(4) Arrangements under sub-paragraph (2) or (3) may provide for the payment of remuneration and allowances to the persons with whom the HRA makes the arrangements.

(5) The HRA may do anything which appears to it to be necessary or desirable for the purposes of or in connection with the exercise of its functions.

Help or advice for other public authorities

14 (1) The HRA may provide help or advice to another public authority for the purpose of the exercise by that authority of its functions.

(2) Help or advice under this paragraph may be provided on such terms as the HRA decides (including terms relating to payment of remuneration and allowances).

(3) "Public authority"—

(a) includes any person certain of whose functions are functions of a public nature, but

(b) does not include either House of Parliament or a person exercising functions in connection with proceedings in Parliament.

(4) A reference to a public authority—

(a) includes a public authority in the Channel Islands or the Isle of Man, but

(b) subject to that, does not include a reference to a public authority outside the United Kingdom.

Arrangements with devolved authorities

15 (1) The HRA may arrange with a devolved authority for the HRA—

(a) to exercise on behalf of the devolved authority any function which corresponds to a function of the HRA;

(b) to provide services or facilities in so far as the devolved authority requires them in connection with the exercise of such a function.

(2) The terms and conditions on which arrangements under this paragraph may be made include provision for payment to the HRA in respect of its costs in giving effect to the arrangements.

Failure to exercise functions

16 (1) If the Secretary of State considers that the HRA is failing or has failed to exercise any of its functions, and that the failure is significant, the Secretary of State may direct the HRA to exercise such of its functions, in such manner and within such period, as the direction specifies.

(2) If the HRA fails to comply with a direction under this paragraph, the Secretary of State may—

(a) exercise the functions specified in the direction, or

(b) make arrangements for some other person to exercise them on the Secretary of State's behalf.

(3) Where the Secretary of State exercises a power under sub-paragraph (1) or (2), the Secretary of State must publish the reasons for doing so.

(4) The reference in sub-paragraph (1) to exercising a function includes a reference to exercising it properly.

PART 3

FINANCE AND REPORTS

Funding

17 The Secretary of State may, with the consent of the Treasury, make payments to the HRA at such times and on such conditions (if any) as the Secretary of State considers appropriate.

Fees and indemnities

18 (1) Regulations may require payment of a fee in relation to the exercise of a specified function of the HRA; and the amount of the fee is to be the amount specified in, or determined in accordance with, the regulations.

(2) Where the amount of a fee is to be specified in regulations under this paragraph—

(a) the Secretary of State must, before specifying the amount of the fee, have regard to the cost incurred in the exercise of the function to which the fee relates, and

(b) the HRA must provide the Secretary of State with such information, in such form, as the Secretary of State may request.

(3) Regulations under this paragraph may require the HRA to determine the amount of a fee; and, where they do so, the regulations—

(a) must require the HRA, before determining the amount of the fee, to have regard to the cost incurred in the exercise of the function to which the fee relates, and

(b) must require the HRA to obtain the approval of the Secretary of State to the proposed amount of the fee.

(4) Regulations under this paragraph which provide for the amount of a fee to be determined may specify factors in accordance with which it is to be determined.

(5) Regulations under this paragraph may include provision—

(a) for determining the time by which a fee is payable;

(b) for any unpaid balance to be recoverable as a debt due to the HRA (but for this not to affect any other method of recovery).

(6) Before making regulations under this paragraph, the Secretary of State must consult such persons as the Secretary of State considers appropriate.

(7) Section 265 of the Public Health Act 1875 (which relates to the protection of members and officers of certain authorities from personal liability) has effect as if there were included in the authorities referred to in that section a reference to the HRA.

(8) In its application to the HRA as a result of sub-paragraph (7), section 265 of that Act has effect as if any reference in that section to that Act were a reference to this Act.

(9) In section 71(2) of the National Health Service Act 2006 (schemes for meeting losses and liabilities etc. of certain health service bodies), after paragraph (f) insert—

"(fa) the Health Research Authority;".

Accounts

19 (1) The HRA must keep accounts in such form as the Secretary of State may determine.

(2) The HRA must prepare annual accounts in respect of each financial year in such form as the Secretary of State may determine.

(3) The HRA must send copies of the annual accounts to—

(a) the Secretary of State, and

(b) the Comptroller and Auditor General,

within such period after the end of the financial year to which the accounts relate as the Secretary of State may determine.

(4) The Comptroller and Auditor General must—

(a) examine, certify and report on the annual accounts, and

(b) lay copies of them and the report on them before Parliament.

(5) In this paragraph and paragraph 20, "financial year" includes the period—

(a) beginning with the day on which the HRA is established, and

(b) ending with the following 31 March or, if the period ending with that date is 3 months or less, ending with the 31 March following that date.

Annual report

20 (1) As soon as is feasible after the end of each financial year, the HRA must prepare an annual report on—

(a) the activities it has undertaken during the year, and

(b) the activities it proposes to undertake during the current financial year.

(2) The report must set out the steps the HRA has taken during the year to fulfil its main objective (see section 110(2)).

(3) The HRA must—

(a) lay a copy of the report before Parliament, and

(b) send a copy of it to the Secretary of State.

(4) The HRA must provide the Secretary of State with such other reports and information relating to the exercise of its functions as the Secretary of State may request.

PART 4

CONSEQUENTIAL AMENDMENTS

Public Records Act 1958

21 In Part 2 of the Table in Schedule 1 to the Public Records Act 1958, at the appropriate place insert—

"Health Research Authority."

Public Bodies (Admission to Meetings) Act 1960

22 In the Schedule to the Public Bodies (Admission to Meetings) Act 1960, after paragraph (bm) (inserted by paragraph 30 of Schedule 5 to this Act) insert—

"(bn) the Health Research Authority;".

Parliamentary Commissioner Act 1967

23 In Schedule 2 to the Parliamentary Commissioner Act 1967, at the appropriate place insert—

"Health Research Authority."

House of Commons Disqualification Act 1975

24 In Part 2 of Schedule 1 to the House of Commons Disqualification Act 1975, at the appropriate place insert—

"The Health Research Authority."

Copyright, Designs and Patents Act 1988

25 In section 48(6) of the Copyright, Designs and Patents Act 1988 (definition of "the Crown"), after "Health Education England" (inserted by paragraph 33 of Schedule 5 to this Act) insert ", the Health Research Authority".

Freedom of Information Act 2000

26 In Part 6 of Schedule 1 to the Freedom of Information Act 2000 (other public bodies), at the appropriate place insert—

"The Health Research Authority."

Equality Act 2010

27 In Part 1 of Schedule 19 to the Equality Act 2010 (authorities subject to the public sector equality duty), in the group of entries under the heading "Health, social care and social security", after the entry for Health Education England (inserted by paragraph 35 of Schedule 5 to this Act) insert—

"The Health Research Authority."

SCHEDULE 8

Section 113

RESEARCH ETHICS COMMITTEES: AMENDMENTS

Ionising Radiation (Medical Exposure) Regulations 2000 (S.I. 2000/1059)

1 In regulation 2(1) of the Ionising Radiation (Medical Exposure) Regulations 2000 (S.I. 2000/1059), in the definition of "ethics committee"—

(a) omit paragraph (a), and

(b) for paragraph (c) substitute—

(c) "a research ethics committee recognised or established by or on behalf of the Health Research Authority under the Care Act 2014, or

(d) any other group of persons which assesses the ethics of research involving individuals and which is recognised for that purpose by or on behalf of the Welsh Ministers or the Scottish Ministers;".

Ionising Radiation (Medical Exposure) Regulations (Northern Ireland) 2000 (S.R. 2000/194)

2 In regulation 2(1) of the Ionising Radiation (Medical Exposure) Regulations (Northern Ireland) 2000 (S.R. 2000/194), for the definition of "ethics committee" substitute—

""ethics committee" means a group of persons which assesses the ethics of research involving individuals and which is recognised for that purpose by or on behalf of the Department;".

Health Service (Control of Patient Information) Regulations 2002 (S.I. 2002/1438)

3 In regulation 1(2) of the Health Service (Control of Patient Information) Regulations 2002 (S.I. 2002/1438), for the definition of "research ethics committee" substitute—

""research ethics committee" means—

(a) a research ethics committee recognised or established by or on behalf of the Health Research Authority under the Care Act 2014, or

(b) any other group of persons which assesses the ethics of research involving individuals and which is recognised for that purpose by or on behalf of the Welsh Ministers."

Nursing Homes Regulations (Northern Ireland) 2005 (S.R. 2005/160)

4 In regulation 2(1) of the Nursing Homes Regulations (Northern Ireland) 2005 (S.R. 2005/160), for the definition of "ethics committee" substitute—

""ethics committee" means a group of persons which assesses the ethics of research involving individuals and which is recognised for that purpose by or on behalf of the Department of Health, Social Services and Public Safety;".

Residential Care Homes Regulations (Northern Ireland) 2005 (S.R. 2005/161)

5 In regulation 2(1) of the Residential Care Homes Regulations (Northern Ireland) 2005 (S.R. 2005/161), for the definition of "ethics committee" substitute—

""ethics committee" means a group of persons which assesses the ethics of research involving individuals and which is recognised for that purpose by or on behalf of the Department of Health, Social Services and Public Safety;".

Independent Health Care Regulations (Northern Ireland) 2005 (S.R. 2005/174)

6 In regulation 2(1) of the Independent Health Care Regulations (Northern Ireland) 2005 (S.R. 2005/174), for the definition of "ethics committee" substitute—

""ethics committee" means a group of persons which assesses the ethics of research involving individuals and which is recognised for that purpose by or on behalf of the Department of Health, Social Services and Public Safety;".

Approval of Research on Organs No Longer Required for Procurator Fiscal Purposes (Specified Purposes) (Scotland) Order 2006 (S.S.I. 2006/310)

7 In article 1(2) of the Approval of Research on Organs No Longer Required for Procurator Fiscal Purposes (Specified Purposes) (Scotland) Order 2006 (S.S.I. 2006/310), for the definition of "appropriate Research Ethics Committee" substitute—

""appropriate Research Ethics Committee" means a group of persons which assesses the ethics of research involving individuals and which is recognised for that purpose by or on behalf of the Scottish Ministers;".

Human Tissue Act 2004 (Ethical Approval, Exceptions from Licensing and Supply of Information about Transplants) Regulations 2006 (S.I. 2006/1260)

8 In regulation 1(2) of the Human Tissue Act 2004 (Ethical Approval, Exceptions from Licensing and Supply of Information about Transplants) Regulations 2006 (S.I. 2006/1260), for the definition of "research ethics authority" substitute—

""research ethics authority" means—

(a) a research ethics committee recognised or established by or on behalf of the Health Research Authority under the Care Act 2014, or

(b) any other group of persons which assesses the ethics of research involving individuals and which is recognised for that purpose by or on behalf of the Welsh Ministers or the Department of Health, Social Services and Public Safety in Northern Ireland."

Mental Capacity Act 2005 (Appropriate Body) (England) Regulations 2006 (S.I. 2006/2810)

9 In regulation 2 of the Mental Capacity Act 2005 (Appropriate Body) (England) Regulations 2006 (S.I. 2006/2810) (definition of "appropriate body"), for the words from "is a committee" to the end substitute "is a research ethics committee recognised or established by or on behalf of the Health Research Authority under the Care Act 2014."

Mental Capacity Act 2005 (Appropriate Body) (Wales) Regulations 2007 (S.I. 2007/833)

10 In regulation 2 of the Mental Capacity 2005 (Appropriate Body) (Wales) Regulations 2007 (S.I. 2007/833) (definition of "appropriate body"), for the words from "is a committee" to the end substitute "is a group of persons which assesses the ethics of research involving individuals and which is recognised for that purpose by or on behalf of the Welsh Ministers."

Human Fertilisation and Embryology (Disclosure of Information for Research Purposes) Regulations 2010 (S.I. 2010/995)

11 In regulation 2(1) of the Human Fertilisation and Embryology (Disclosure of Information for Research Purposes) Regulations 2010 (S.I. 2010/995), for the definition of "research ethics committee" substitute—

> ""research ethics committee" means a research ethics committee recognised or established by or on behalf of the Health Research Authority under the Care Act 2014;".

Independent Health Care (Wales) Regulations 2011 (S.I. 2011/734)

12 In regulation 25 of the Independent Health Care (Wales) Regulations 2011 (S.I. 2011/734) (research), in paragraph (2) for the words from "a research ethics committee" to the end substitute "a group of persons which assesses the ethics of research involving individuals and which is recognised for that purpose by or on behalf of the Welsh Ministers."

GRANGIS - UK PUBLISHING 2022.

www.ingramcontent.com/pod-product-compliance
Lightning Source LLC
LaVergne TN
LVHW060212210926
848481LV00008B/2710